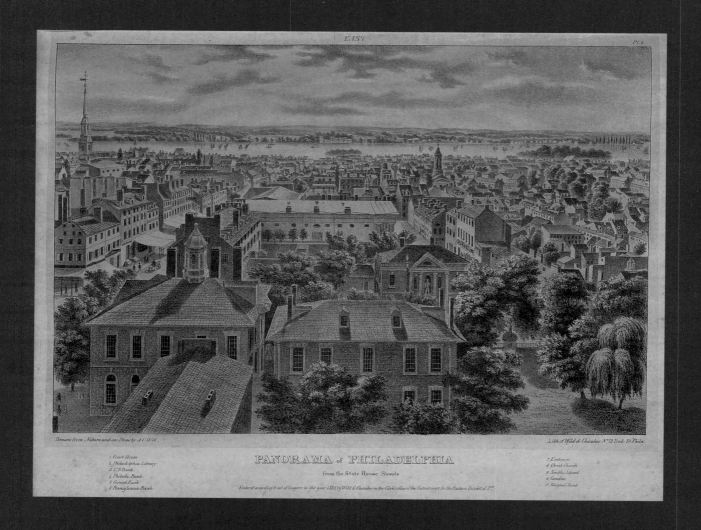

PANORAMA of PHILADELPHIA

from the State House Steeple

Drawn from Nature and on Stone by J. C. Wild

Lith. of Wild & Chevalier N.º 72 Dock St. Phila.

1 Court House
2 Philadelphia Library
3 U.S. Bank
4 Philada. Bank
5 Girard Bank
6 Pennsylvania Bank

7 Exchange
8 Christ Church
9 Smiths Island
10 Camden
11 Kaighns Point

Entered according to act of Congress in the year 1838 by Wild & Chevalier in the Clerk's office of the District court for the Eastern District of Pa.

"The story of this remarkable enterprise begins in Philadelphia.
Indeed, as far as these collectors were concerned,
it was as though the whole world was Philadelphia.
But it did not remain that way for long.
The collection soon expanded and reached beyond the narrow confines
of a single city. In time it came to embrace the entire nation."

from the Historical Overview, page 2

GATHERING HISTORY

The Marian S. Carson Collection of Americana

Historical Overview by

Robert V. Remini

With essays by

Gerard W. Gawalt

Carol Johnson

Harry L. Katz

and

Rosemary Fry Plakas

Edited by

Sara Day

Library of Congress, Washington 1999

**Frontispiece: John Caspar Wild. "Panorama of Philadelphia,"
color lithograph, 1838. See page 2.**

**Front endpaper: John Rubens Smith after John Rowson Smith.
View of Pottsville. Etching with aquatint and watercolor, 1833.
See page 84.**

**Back endpaper: Theo. E. Peiser. Seattle's first street car turning
from Occidental Avenue to Yesler Way. Albumen silver print, 1884.
See page 114.**

This publication was made possible by generous support from the James
Madison Council, a national, private-sector advisory council dedicated to
helping the Library of Congress share its unique resources with the nation
and the world.

Library of Congress Cataloging-in-Publication Data

Marian S. Carson Collection (Library of Congress)
Gathering history: the Marian S. Carson collection of Americana
/historical overview by Robert V. Remini;
with essays by Gerard W. Gawalt . . . [et al.]. :
edited by Sara Day.

p.   cm.
Includes bibliographical references and index.

ISBN 0-8444-0977-4 (pbk. : alk. paper)
Copy 3 Z663.7 .G58 1999

1. United States—Civilization—Library resources.
2. Philadelphia (Pa.)—Civilization—Library resources.
3. Americana—Private collections—Washington (D.C.)
4. Carson, Marian S.—Library.
5. Carson, Marian S.—Art collections.
6. Carson, Marian S.—Photograph collections.
7. Library resources—Washington (D.C.)
8. Library of Congress.
I. Remini, Robert Vincent, 1921- .
II. Gawalt, Gerard W.
III. Day, Sara, 1943- .

Z12. I.G38   1999
016.973—DC21

98-51398
CIP

Director of Publishing, Library of Congress: W. Ralph Eubanks
Production Manager, Library of Congress: Gloria Baskerville-Holmes

Design: Garruba|Dennis|Konetzka, Washington, D.C.

For sale by the Superintendent of Documents,
U.S. Government Printing Office, Washington, D.C. 20402

Contents

Preface

The Library of Congress, which celebrates its bicentennial in the year 2000, has acquired more than 115 million items in its long and distinguished history, including numerous collections of great import and impressive scope. Few, however, approach the scale and historic significance of the Marian S. Carson Collection. Encompassing more than 10,000 manuscripts, photographs, prints, drawings, books, and broadsides from the Colonial era through the 1876 Centennial celebration it represents, quite simply, the Library's most significant acquisition of Americana in this century.

Dr. James H. Billington and Mrs. Marian S. Carson at the celebration marking the acquisition of the Carson Collection, Library of Congress, October 1996. Photograph by Neshan H. Naltchayan.

The collection was formed by Philadelphia resident Marian Carson and several equally prescient members of her family, including her grandfather Julius F. Sachse, an author, antiquarian, and dedicated amateur photographer; her father-in-law Hampton L. Carson, attorney general of Pennsylvania and U.S. Supreme Court historian; and her husband Joseph Carson, bibliophile and avid collector of prints, books, and manuscripts. They shared through generations an extraordinary passion for the written and

visual artifacts of American history and amassed the largest private collection of its kind in the nation.

In her own collecting activities Mrs. Carson added substantially to the holdings her family had already begun to build, ranging far and wide in pursuit of a rare and intriguing item: "If someone told me of a shop in Charleston or up in western Massachusetts I was there within 24 hours," she told Library curators in 1998. A native Philadelphian, she focused her collecting on that city's central role in the founding and formation of the American republic. In addition, she gathered pamphlets, letters, ledgers, invoices, and other ephemera related to such broad topics as women, religion, slavery, education, and medicine in the eighteenth and nineteenth centuries. Armed with keen curatorial instincts and profound antiquarian interest she acquired countless apparently mundane items which another collector might eschew. Research value, not aesthetic or financial concerns, guided her quest. She pursued this quest with catholic tastes and disarming spontaneity, purchasing one item only to find it might lead her toward another. There are few aspects of the country's growth between 1776 and 1876 that are not in some way touched upon in this remarkable collection.

Among its highlights are a 1775 handwritten list of the Pennsylvania Germans who sent funds in support of Bostonians impoverished by the British embargo; a book once owned, held, and cherished by Martha Washington; the first photographic portrait taken in America; an 1856 watercolor of the newly formed Liberian Senate; a letter penned by an eyewitness to an early foray of the Pony Express; and numerous, delicate eighteenth- and nineteenth-century children's books and games. These items possess their own separate dignity, yet seen collectively they are awesome to behold.

The Carson Collection contains vast amounts of historical raw material, largely unplumbed and awaiting the interest and energy of researchers. Through its

The Carson Collection contains vast amounts of historical raw material, largely unplumbed and awaiting the interest and energy of researchers... the Library of Congress has already begun to make these materials available, both physically on Capitol Hill and electronically through the Internet, to an international audience of students and scholars.

state-of-the-art preservation and cataloging programs, the Library of Congress has already begun to make these materials available, both physically on Capitol Hill and electronically through the Internet, to an international audience of students and scholars. With the advent of this new, constantly shifting virtual environment, such tangible yet fragile documents and artifacts become ever more precious as the master records of our nation's heritage. We are proud to have acquired, and honored to preserve, this magnificent legacy which Marian Carson and her family labored over several lifetimes to create.

In preparing this book, we called on Library specialists who have worked closely with Marian Carson and her collection to guide us through its major strengths and share with us their expertise and insights. Professor Robert Remini's lively and informative introduction brings this multitude of rare books, drawings, and manuscripts to vivid life, and we are very appreciative of his contribution. We also want to extend enormous gratitude to the Library's James Madison Council—and in particular to David Koch, James and Margaret Elkins, Charles and Norma Dana, and the council's chairman John W. Kluge—for their munificent support toward the acquisition of a large portion of the Carson Collection and the publication of this book.

Finally, we wish to acknowledge the generosity of Marian Carson and her family. We are particularly grateful to her daughters, Lea Sherk and Wynne Curry, who were instrumental in undertaking the difficult task of transferring the collection from her townhouse in Philadelphia. We are extremely gratified by Marian Carson's decision to place the collection at the Library and, on behalf of the nation's scholars, thank her for her long and responsible stewardship of this archives. Her efforts are in the best traditions of American scholarship and antiquarianism. In recognition of her achievement we have named her the honorary curator of the Carson Collection of Americana. This acquisition marks the culmination of her lifelong search for the next great find, the next rare nugget of historical interest, preserved for the future and now given to the nation.

James H. Billington
The Librarian of Congress

Acknowledgments

Mrs. Carson's decision to entrust her collection to the Library of Congress followed several years of discussions with Bernard F. Reilly, former Head Curator of the Prints and Photographs Division and now Director of Research at the Chicago Historical Society, and members of his staff at that time, particularly Harry L. Katz, Curator of Popular and Applied Graphic Art, and Carol Johnson, Assistant Curator of Photography.

Harry Katz, who led the initial planning for this book, wishes to thank Director of Publishing Ralph Eubanks and Linda Ayres, Chief of the Prints and Photographs Division, for their constant support and invaluable expertise, as well as Nancy Glanville and Carter Smith of the James Madison Council for their early advice and encouragement. Professor Robert Remini acknowledges with profound thanks the help of editor Sara Day, who not only provided documents for his historical overview but also information on Mrs. Carson's family gathered by her in Philadelphia and at the Library. He is also grateful to Bernard Reilly for his account of the acquisition and the collection and to the specialists for allowing him to examine their parts of the collection and explaining the importance of individual items. Sara Day thanks Lea Sherk for verifying aspects of the collecting history.

For providing information for his essay, Harry Katz thanks Don Cresswell, Philadelphia Print Shop; Donald O'Brien, American Historical Print Collectors Society; Sylvia Yount, Pennsylvania Academy of the Fine Arts; Sally Pierce, Boston Athenaeum; and Dale Biever, Civil War Library and Museum, Philadelphia. Gerard W. Gawalt, Manuscript Historian, would like to thank Margit H. Kerwin, archivist in the Manuscript Division, for her assistance in identifying and locating materials in the Carson Collection. Rosemary Plakas appreciates the support and thoughtful suggestions of Mark Dimunation, Chief, Rare Book and Special Collections Division, and the special assistance of Jacqueline Coleburn and Thomas Bishop. Carol Johnson is grateful to Marcy Silver Flynn for valuable information about the contributions of Julius F. Sachse to the history of photography and to Mary Jane Appel for her thoughtful editorial comments.

Behind the words of the historians and specialists who describe the riches of the Marian S. Carson Collection are the efforts of staff members who have spent many hours working to ensure that the collection is preserved and made accessible. An unprecedented number of individual items from the collection have received expert attention by the staff of the Conservation Division, including Sylvia Albro, Marita Clance, Carol Crawford, Jeff Dunbar, Judith Emprechtiger, Annlinn Grossmann, Alan Haley, Yasmeen Khan, Holly Krueger, Nancy Lev-Alexander, Kate Morrison, Andrew Robb, and Ann Seibert, under the direction of Doris A. Hamburg, head, Preventive Preservation Section, and Thomas C. Albro II, head, Book and Paper Section. The collection has been organized and cataloged by professionals in each of the major divisions responsible for special formats: for the Manuscript Division, archivist Margit Kerwin; for the Rare Book and Special Collections Division, Thomas Bishop, Jacqueline Coleburn, David Kennaly, and Jiping Wu of the Rare Book Team, Special Materials Cataloging Division; for the Prints and Photographs Division, Woody Woodis, Brett Carnell, and Gregory Marcangelo.

Well over one hundred treasures from the Collection were carefully and expeditiously photographed by the Library's photographers, Yusef El Amin and James R. Higgins, Jr., after being retrieved from custodial divisions by Yvonne Brooks, Margaret Kieckhefer, and Georgia Zola. Freelance museum photographer Edward Owen worked with the curators to photograph items requiring special attention and lighting. The photographers' work has provided the visual dimension for the two sides of Mrs. Carson's vision, the documents themselves and the knowledge that they impart.

John Rubens Smith, model drawings of household vessels,
lithograph from Smith, *The Juvenile Drawing-Book* (Philadelphia, 1854).
Rare Book and Special Collections Division, Library of Congress.

Historical Overview

by Robert V. Remini

Professor Emeritus of History, University of Illinois at Chicago

OPPOSITE

(detail) P.S. Duval & Son after James Queen, *Star Spangled Banner.* Chromolithograph on paper, 1861. See page 13.

It is a rare event these days for an American historian to come across a huge collection of documentary material, running to more than 10,000 items, that illuminates numerous aspects of American history and has been hitherto seen by a very few people. Such an event occurred in 1996 when the Library of Congress acquired Marian S. Carson's vast collection of Americana.

The extraordinary size of this collection can be explained by the fact that it is not the collection of a single individual. Actually it is many collections, certainly five or six, perhaps more, and represents several lifetimes of collecting. It constitutes the efforts of a group of individuals, in particular Marian and Joseph Carson and their forebears, whose passion for collecting—and collecting what pertained principally to American life and society—bordered on obsession.

Between them, they amassed an extraordinary variety of objects and materials: furniture, china, silver, paintings, prints and drawings, early daguerreotypes and photographs, manuscripts, books, pamphlets, broadsides, and related ephemera of every description. However, it should be stated clearly at the outset that from this sumptuous horde the Library of Congress acquired principally those works that were on paper, plus glass plate negatives, of which the Library of Congress has already acquired large collections, and a small oil painting on panel by Henry Inman.

The story of this remarkable enterprise begins in Philadelphia. Indeed, as far as these collectors were concerned, it was as though the whole world was Philadelphia. But it did not remain that way for long. The collection soon expanded and reached beyond the narrow confines of a single city. In time it came to embrace the entire nation.

Joseph and Marian Carson were the children and grandchildren of collectors and over a period of time they individually built separate but related collections. What undoubtedly spurred their initial interest in Americana, apart from family tradition, was the rediscovery by historians, sociologists, literary critics, artists, and others in the 1920s and 1930s that the nation had a cultural as well as an historical past that deserved preservation and study. The sesquicentennial celebrations of the Declaration of Independence in Philadelphia in 1926; the restoration of colonial buildings in historic down-town Philadelphia; the establishment of the Independence National Historical Park, in which the Carsons were involved in the planning stages and loaned materials for the exhibitions; the restoration and opening to public viewing of colonial houses, such as Thomas Jefferson's Monticello, those in Colonial Williamsburg, and the Colonial Chain of Houses in Fairmount Park in Philadelphia; the opening in 1924 of the American wing of decorative arts in the traditional, Eurocentric Metropolitan Museum of Art

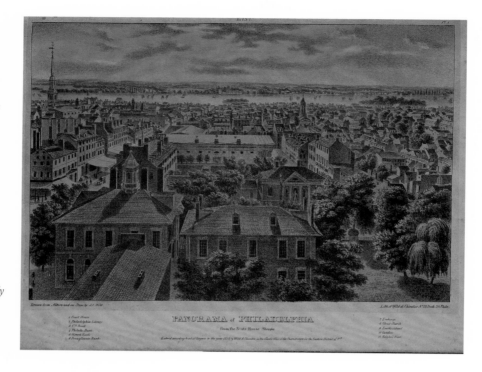

For more than forty years, Mrs. Carson lived a block or two from Independence Hall (formerly the State House), in the heart of Colonial Philadelphia, and was actively involved in the Independence National Historical Park project. Wild's panorama east from the State House shows other historic landmarks, including, in the foreground, Old City Hall, the east wing of the State House, and Philosophical Hall. Behind them are the colonnaded Library Hall and the imposing Second Bank of the United States. Further east are the small cupolaed Carpenters' Hall, the colonnaded First Bank of the United States, and the large cupolaed Merchants' Exchange. At the left soars the steeple of Christ Church.

in New York; and the establishment of new museums of Americana, such as the Museum and Greenfield Village in Dearborn, Michigan, that Henry Ford opened in 1929—these and more sparked a heightened consciousness of the importance and value of American culture. All of which most likely spurred the Carsons to acquire, preserve, and study artifacts of the nation's past, whether they dealt with furniture, houses, shipbuilding, the postal system, engineering, gambling, sports, city planning, painting, or documents relating to the lives of ordinary people.

Marian Carson's collecting in Americana had its genesis in the decorative arts, specifically Philadelphia furniture. Following her marriage in the early 1920s, she assisted her first husband, William Macpherson Hornor, Jr., in the compilation of his authoritative *Blue Book Philadelphia Furniture: William Penn to George Washington* (1935), which pictured more than five hundred pieces of furniture held by prominent members of Philadelphia families and handed down from generation to generation. As she stated in the preface of the 1977 reissue of this publication, the

time had arrived "for a new breed of informed collector," one whose labors would include "research, public forums, restoration, and publications," not simply acquisition.[1]

From 1935 on she acted out her creed and widened her interests to include historical prints and drawings—obtaining the James Queen and John Rubens Smith archives—and early daguerreotypes and paper photographs. Through an aunt, she inherited a portion of the photographic collection of her late grandfather, Dr. Julius F. Sachse. With her subsequent marriage to Joseph Carson in 1942, Marian not only moved into a rambling farmhouse in Bryn Mawr that was filled with beautiful paintings, prints, books, china, and furniture, but she became strongly influenced by her husband's belief in and commitment to social history.

Among his many other civic posts, Joseph Carson was a member of the Council of the Historical Society of Pennsylvania and served on a committee with six other men, including Julian P. Boyd, the distinguished librarian and editor, in drawing up a

James Queen, Firehouse scene. Watercolor on paper, ca. 1857. Prints and Photographs Division, Library of Congress (LC-USZC4-6029).

Great urban conflagrations occurred regularly in America during the nineteenth century and firemen were celebrated in countless popular prints from the period. James Queen's fire-related images are particularly noteworthy for the realism he achieved through his own experience as a fireman with Philadelphia's Weccacoe Volunteer Company. At this time, there were forty-five engine-, forty-two hose-, and five ladder-companies in the city.

statement of objectives for the Historical Society. The result was a declaration of policy that announced "a belief in the value and dignity of the incomparable story of America, a delight in its variant voices from all lands blending into a common voice of hope and promise." The statement further declared that the Society had "a deep concern for the life of the people as well as a desire to record the actions of their leaders." It affirmed that "here in Pennsylvania—from the beginning the most cosmopolitan and democratic of all the States—history concerns itself with the Finns and Swedes, the Dutch and English, the Scots-Irish and Germans, the Negroes and Slavs, without regard to their status, their beliefs, their color, their accent." There must be, it continued, a "broad and intelligent interest in the fundamental unit in society, the family." The role of the family had in the past and would continue in the future to play an important role in the Society's activities and interests, "and not a mere concern for the compilation of genealogical tables." The statement concluded by declaring a formal abandonment of the "warehouse theory of custodianship;

it substitutes therefor [sic] a trusteeship, to be justified only in terms of increased accessibility and increased usefulness." Such a policy can only enhance "the great drama that is American history."[2]

Marian Carson clearly shared this belief and commitment. In her article, "Philadelphia a Century Ago," published in *The American Philatelist*, in which she spoke about the several hundred pictures she loaned for the centenary commemoration of a new series of U.S. stamps authorized by Congress, she stated that the pictures "were the result of many years of study and collecting … Mr. Carson, more than anyone else I know," she wrote, "appreciates the wealth of social and economic history such pictures reflect." As a result of this concern Marian Carson herself further broadened her collecting interests to include education, law, transportation, trade, manufacturing, labor, shipping, medicine, women, African-Americans, Native Americans, children, and many other topics of the American past.

In this same article she went on to acknowledge the collecting done by her husband's father, Hampton L. Carson, an attorney-general of Pennsylvania (1903-07) and author of *The History of the Supreme Court of the United States (1902),* among other legal and historical works, and the several collections he acquired of portraits, prints, and documents in the

field of Americana, that he later sold or gave to the Free Library of Philadelphia. Continuing on the Carson side, she saluted the work of her husband's grandfather, Dr. Joseph Carson, a distinguished Philadelphia physician who wrote the widely admired *History of the Medical Department of the University of Pennsylvania* (1869) and who achieved a reputation as a respected antiquarian. Marian Carson also acknowledged that her own collecting was "part of a serious study of Philadelphia's economic and social past" in all its many forms and expressions, and that her parents had made her conscious of the "charm and interest in the antique." Her grandfather, Dr. Julius F. Sachse, author of books and articles on masonry, German pietism, the music of the Ephrata Cloister, Pennsylvania German history, and other subjects had been "indefatigable," she said, in collecting books, pamphlets, pictures, and historical documents. And indeed Sachse was one of the first men to recognize the importance of photography, "a subject his father had had a part in as early as 1840."[3]

Following her husband's death in 1953, Marian Carson moved with her daughters to an historic house on Washington Square in downtown Society Hill, the very epicenter of Colonial Philadelphia history, to continue her work collecting Americana. This collection, then, began as the Philadelphia/

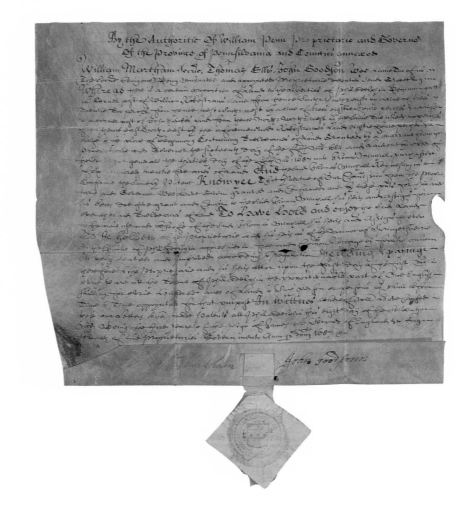

Pennsylvania story, and little of that story apparently was overlooked in the massive amounts of manuscripts, pictorial matter, and books acquired, most of which now reside in the Library of Congress. And that is where this introduction to the Carson Collection should begin.

William Penn, a young friend of Charles II of England, received a royal charter from the king in 1681 to discharge a debt of £16,000 owed by the monarch to Penn's father, Admiral William Penn, by which he became the proprietor for a huge tract of land in what is roughly now the state of Pennsylvania. While a student at Oxford, Penn had been converted to the beliefs of the Society of Friends, or Quakers, served a prison sentence for his beliefs, and upon his release traveled as a missionary to Holland and Germany, where he organized Quaker societies. The Society of Friends obeyed only the "inner light" of conscience, not the authority of ministers, priests, or bishops. They believed in complete equality, would not bow or kneel or remove their hats, even before the king's officials, and opposed violence and war.

The Waln family of prominent
Quaker merchants and
manufacturers had provided
civic and economic leadership
in Philadelphia for several
generations before Robert
Waln, Jr., while still in his
twenties, offered these satirical
observations on the manners
of Philadelphia society,
including "some account
of the human leeches, belles,
beaux, coquettes, dandies,
cotillion parties, supper
parties, tea parties, &c. &c.
of that famous city...."
His more serious publications
included a history of
China and biographies of
Lafayette and several of the
signers of the Declaration
of Independence.

Despite his membership in this "radical sect" and his own imprisonment, Penn maintained his friendship with Charles II and, with the grant given him, planned to establish a haven for persecuted Quakers. It would be a "holy experiment," providing a model of amity and harmony for all, a model of religious liberty and Christian living. Both the "Frame of Government" and the Code of Laws adopted for Pennsylvania reflected the founder's liberal views by guaranteeing open courts, jury trials, and speedy justice. At a time when minor offenses could be punished by death in England, in this new colony only murder and treason were designated as capital crimes. Penn also made every effort to treat Native Americans fairly and protect them from the rapacious land hunger of white settlers.

Penn demonstrated considerable organizing skill in attracting Europeans to his colony. He advertised his province in handsomely produced pamphlets and distributed them both on the Continent and in England. Land was offered at extremely low prices and rents started for as little as a penny an acre. Settlers poured into the colony, not only persecuted English Quakers looking for sanctuary, but immigrants from France, Sweden, Holland, and Germany. Of particular importance were the many shopkeepers, merchants, and skilled artisans who flocked to Pennsylvania.

The year following the granting of the charter for this proprietary colony Penn himself came to America and laid out the town of Philadelphia—the City of Brotherly Love, as he called it—a rectangular tract of 1,200 acres extending from the Delaware to the Schuylkill Rivers. Mercantile trade became the bedrock of the city's economy and by the end of the seventeenth century Philadelphia enjoyed a population of 2,200, living in 400 houses. By the end of the next century it had surpassed New York and Boston as the leading metropolitan area among the colonies.

Many Quaker families played an extremely important role in the development and prosperity of both the city and the colony, not only as traders and merchants but as lawyers, doctors, bankers, legislative leaders, educators, and philanthropists. They helped convert Philadelphia from a thriving commercial

From the Monthly Meeting of FRIENDS,

Called by Some

The FREE QUAKERS,

Held by Adjournment at Philadelphia, on the 9th Day of the 7th Month, 1781.

To those of our Brethren who have disowned us.

BRETHREN,

AMONG the very great number of persons whom you have disowned for matters religious and civil, a number have felt a necessity of uniting together for the discharge of those religious duties, which we undoubtedly owe to God and to one another. We have accordingly met and having seriously considered our situation, agreed to establish and endeavour to support, on the ancient and sure foundation, meetings for public worship, and meetings for conducting our religious affairs. And we rejoice in a firm hope, that as we humble ourselves before God, his presence will be found in them, and his blessing descend and rest upon them.

As you have by your proceedings against us separated yourselves from us, and declared that you have no unity with us, you have compelled us, however unwillingly, to become separate from you. And we are free to declare to you and to the world, that we are not desirous of having any mistake which we may happen to make laid to your charge; neither are we willing to have any of your errors brought as guilt against us. To avoid these, seeing that you have made the separation, we submit to have a plain line of distinction drawn between us and you. But there are some points which seem to require a comparison of sentiment between you and us, and some kind of decision to be made upon them. The property of that society of which we and you were once joint members, is far from being inconsiderable, and we have done nothing which can afford even a pretension of our having forfeited our right therein.

Whether you have or have not a right to declare to the world your sentiments of the conduct of any individual: Or whether you have or have not a right to sit in judgment over and pass sentence upon your christian brethren differing in sentiment from you, although educated among you, are not questions now to be considered : But you having taken upon you to do those things, it remains only to be enquired, What are the consequences in law and equity of your having so done. Surely you will not pretend that *our right* is destroyed by those *acts of yours*. But we suggest to your consideration, Whether your conduct has or has not in law, disqualified you to hold any part of that property ? A serious and full consideration of this question, and the critical and strikingly singular situation in which you stand, cannot injure you ; but it may, possibly, induce you to consider, with the more candour and readiness, what equity requires to be done by you toward us, or by us toward you. And tend to a decision the most proper between brethren, differing in sentiment one from another concerning their respective rights to property, yet each believing in him whose precepts leads us to " do unto others as we would they should do unto us."

Whatever may have been the consequences to yourselves, either of your conduct toward us as friends to the present revolution ; or of your conduct in other cases, less immediately respecting us, it seems to be unquestionably certain, that *we* have not done any thing which can possibly forfeit *our right*. And we see no reason why we should surrender it up to you ; but think it a duty incumbent on us to assert our claim.

As a place for holding our meetings for worship, and meetings for business relative to the society is become necessary for us, since you have separated yourselves from us, by testifying against us, and thereby rendering it highly improper for us to appear among you, as one people, at your meetings, we think it proper for us to use, apart from you, one of the houses built by friends in this city for those purposes. We are desirous of doing this in the most decent and unexceptionable manner, and are willing to hear any thing which you may chuse to say on the subject : And, therefore, we thus invite you to the opportunity of doing it, and of shewing what degree of kindness and brotherly love toward us, still remains among you. We also mean to use the burial ground, whenever the occasion shall require it : For, however the living may contend, surely the dead may lie peaceably together.

Lest any may infer too much from this representation, we think it proper explicitly to declare, that should our right to the property in question be found, in the law, to be superior to yours, from any consideration whatever, it is far, very far from our wish to seclude you from a joint participation with us in the use of it : Neither do we mean to solicit a decision in law, unless you by your conduct compel us to it.

We sincerely and earnestly desire to have this subject amicably, equitably and speedily adjusted, and request that this free communication of our sentiments may be made known to all who are usually consulted on business among you, and that, for this purpose, it may be read when you next meet together on religious business.

As Christians, labouring in some degree to forgive injuries, we salute you, and, though disowned and rejected by you, we are your friends and brethren.

Signed in, and on behalf of the said Meeting, by

SAMUEL WETHERILL, jun. CLERK.

H 4104

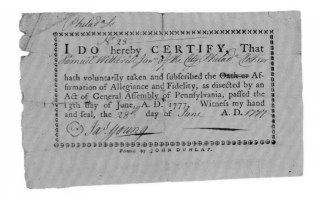

Philadᵃ

Nᵒ 28

I DO hereby CERTIFY, That Samuel Wetherill Junʳ of the City Philadᵃ ~~~ hath voluntarily taken and subscribed the ~~Oath or~~ Affirmation of Allegiance and Fidelity, as directed by an Act of General Assembly of Pennsylvania, passed the 13th day of June, A. D. 1777, Witness my hand and seal, the 28ᵗ day of June A. D. 1777

Saml Young

Printed by JOHN DUNLAP.

ABOVE

Samuel Wetherill, Jr., affirmation of allegiance, June 28, 1777. Manuscript Division, Library of Congress.

Since Quakers were forbidden from taking oaths, they scratched that word from the allegiance documents that all Pennsylvanians were required to sign following adoption of the Declaration of Independence. The future leader of the Free Quakers was at this time calling himself "junior" in deference to his father of the same name.

LEFT

Samuel Wetherill, Jr., Clerk, *From the Monthly Meeting of Friends, Called by Some The Free Quakers*, broadside, July 9, 1781. Manuscript Division, Library of Congress.

Having been disowned by the Society of Friends, the so-called Free Quakers, under the leadership of Samuel Wetherill, announced their intention to worship separately from the main body of Friends in Philadelphia, although they would continue to use the regular Quaker burial ground

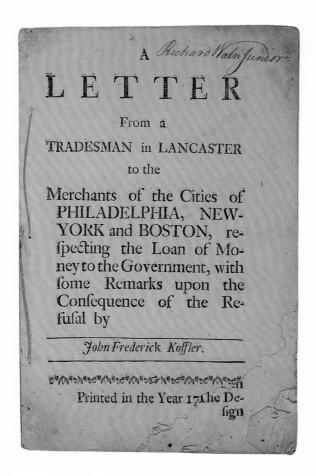

A

LETTER

From a

TRADESMAN in LANCASTER

to the

Merchants of the Cities of
PHILADELPHIA, NEW-
YORK and BOSTON, re-
specting the Loan of Mo-
ney to the Government, with
some Remarks upon the
Consequence of the Re-
fusal by

John Frederick Koffler.

Printed in the Year 171he Design

**John Frederick Koffler, *A Letter From a Tradesman
in Lancaster to the Merchants of the Cities of
Philadelphia, New-York and Boston, respecting the Loan
of Money to the Government* (Lancaster, Pennsylvania,
1760). Rare Book and Special Collections Division,
Library of Congress.**

*This rare financial treatise is inscribed and dated April 11, 1760,
by the Philadelphia Quaker merchant Richard Waln, Jr.,
whose family papers were diligently sought by the Carsons. In
his treatise, Koffler expresses his concerns for Philadelphia
merchants, including their lending money to the government
and accumulating debt, and sternly warns against their going
into the insurance business.*

mart into the center of political, social, cultural, and economic life in the American colonies. The Carson Collection contains the papers of many of these families, along with documents pertaining to William Penn and his descendants, the study of which should prove extremely enlightening to historians in understanding colonial life and how it evolved.

With the outbreak of the American Revolution, the Quaker sect tried to remain neutral but a good number of them sided with the patriot cause and were ostracized by the more traditional members of the Society of Friends. The Free Quakers, as they came to be called, helped advance the revolutionary cause with whatever means they had, including food, clothing, and manufactured goods, and several members served as quartermasters and commissaries

for the army. They maintained their separate identity well into the nineteenth century and built a Free Quaker Meeting House in the 1780s close to Independence Hall in Philadelphia, architectural drawings of which are among the papers of the Carson Collection.

The families of these Free Quakers, including the often interrelated Hornors, Coates, Wetherills, Bringhursts, Yarnalls, Walns, and Cressons, kept extensive papers which document the activities of their sect as well as life in Pennsylvania. Joseph and Marian Carson took particular pains to collect these family papers and, brought together into one collection, they throw considerable light on business affairs, government, religion, education, and political developments at the turn of the nineteenth century.

William Shippen, Jr., memorandum notes, 1791.
Manuscript Division, Library of Congress.

William Shippen, Jr., Philadelphia physician, made a note of patients treated by him one summer day in 1791, including both President Washington and Secretary of State Jefferson. The evocative sheet is representative of Mrs. Carson's interest in collecting documentation of early medical history.

Quakers were especially interested in education, as were the Carsons, and a running story of education in America can be gleaned from these papers, books, pamphlets, and ephemera. Medicine was another special interest in a city renowned for its leadership in the field. The record book of Dr. William Shippen, Jr. shows that he counted Thomas Jefferson and "the President," George Washington, among his patients. A rare medical book in this collection, *A Syllabus of a Course of Lectures on the Institutes of Medicine*, was published in 1795 by Benjamin Rush, probably the most distinguished physician of his time. In the book the good doctor discourses on "the peculiarities of the male and female body and mind" as well as menstruation, conception and parturition, the circulation of blood, the nervous system, senses, and the faculties and operations of the brain.[4]

Political life in America centered in Philadelphia following the outbreak of the Revolution, as evidenced by the adoption of the Declaration of Independence and the writing of the Constitution. Once the colonies had declared their liberation from Great Britain, Pennsylvanians by statute were required to sign an oath of allegiance. Because their religious beliefs forbade them from taking an oath, Quakers struck out the offending word from the document in favor of the word "affirmation." As signed by each Quaker the text was changed to read, "I do hereby certify that [name of individual] hath voluntarily taken and subscribed the affirmation of allegiance and fidelity, as directed by an Act of General Assembly of Pennsylvania...." Copies of these documents can be found among the Carson papers.

Following the ratification of the Constitution in 1788, the capital of the United States moved temporarily to New York, but returned to Philadelphia in 1790 where it remained for a decade until it moved to Washington, D.C., in 1800. Most of the administrations of George Washington and John Adams played out in the City of Brotherly Love. It was here that the two-party system was first developed, the national debt was funded, a national bank was established, and a judicial system was put in place that to this

Frontifpeice -

The Marquifs of Satstars Obfervatory

THE
NEWTONIAN SYSTEM
OF
PHILOSOPHY.
Adapted to the Capacities of
YOUNG LADIES AND GENTLEMEN,
And familiarized and made entertaining,
By Objects with which they are inti-
mately acquainted:
Being the Subftance of Six Lectures,
Read to a Select Company of Friends,
BY TOM TELESCOPE, A. M.
First collected and methodized by the late Mr.
Newberry, for the Instruction and rational Enter-
tainment of the Youth of these Kingdoms.

Illustrated with Copperplates.

A NEW EDITION,
Revised and enriched by an Account of the late new
Philosophical Discoveries,
BY WILLIAM MAGNET, F. L. S.

LONDON:
Printed for OGILVY and SPEARE, Middle-Row,
HOLBORN. 1794.
Price One Shilling and Sixpence bound.

Tom Telescope, A.M.,
*The Newtonian System
of Philosophy Adapted to
the Capacities of Young
Ladies and Gentlemen*
(London, 1794).
Rare Book and Special
Collections Division,
Library of Congress.
*Presented in the
fictionalized framework
of a holiday adventure by
Tom Telescope and his school
friends to the observatory
of the Marquis of Setstar,
these simplified scientific
lectures on the universe
transcend school lessons to
become entertainment. In
1817 Thomas Birch owned
this copy of the popular
instructional work attributed
to Oliver Goldsmith. The
British-born artist of land-
and marinescapes, son of
William Birch, had recently
completed four years as
curator of the Pennsylvania
Academy of Fine Arts.*

Henry Inman, Head of Columbia. Oil on panel, ca. 1830s. Prints and Photographs Division, Library of Congress. Photograph by Edward Owen.

During the nineteenth century such talented American artists as Henry Inman supplemented their production of portraits and historical paintings with designs for state seals, coins, certificates, and banknotes, thus blurring the distinction between fine and applied art.

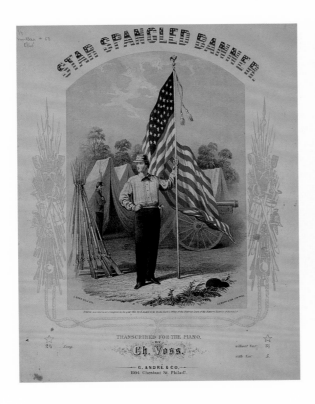

day remains the basic legal structure of the country. Joseph Hopkinson, a noted Philadelphia jurist, composed "Hail Columbia" in 1798, which for many years served as the veritable national anthem before the "Star Spangled Banner" replaced it. Several of his father Francis Hopkinson's musical compositions are contained in the Carson Collection, including a toast to George Washington (see pages 44 and 45).

Although Washington, D.C., had become the capital and the center of political power in the country, Philadelphia continued to occupy an important position in business, manufacturing, law, medicine, education, cultural affairs, religion, philanthropy, and politics, and the Carsons continued acquiring memorabilia that documented those areas. But now their active interests moved beyond Philadelphia and Pennsylvania and extended across the rest of the country. Now their outlook became truly national and even stretched overseas, wherever American interests were involved.

John Yarnall to uncle (Samuel Wetherill, Jr.), Sandwich Isles, Woahoo, August 4, 1810. Manuscript Division, Library of Congress.

Philadelphia merchant John Yarnall was among the first Americans to report from the Sandwich Islands (the name given to them by their discoverer Captain James Cook) during their first year as the united and independent kingdom of Hawaii under King Kamehameha I. Tragically, the native population of these remote islands was greatly reduced by the devastating infectious diseases brought by American and European traders.

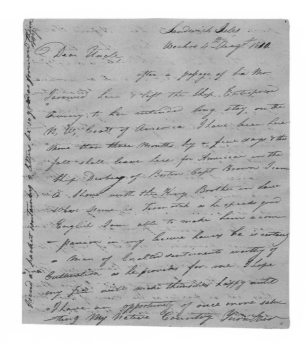

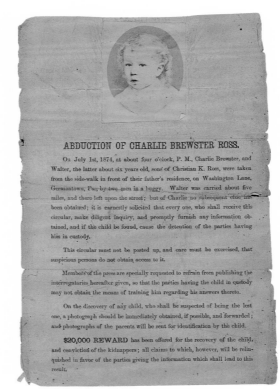

ABDUCTION OF CHARLIE BREWSTER ROSS.

On July 1st, 1874, at about four o'clock, P. M., Charlie Brewster, and Walter, the latter about six years old, sons of Christian K. Ross, were taken from the side-walk in front of their father's residence, on Washington Lane, Germantown, Pa.; by two men in a buggy. Walter was carried about five miles, and there left upon the street; but of Charlie no subsequent clue has been obtained; it is earnestly solicited that every one, who shall receive this circular, make diligent inquiry, and promptly furnish any information obtained, and if the child be found, cause the detention of the parties having him in custody.

This circular must not be posted up, and care must be exercised, that suspicious persons do not obtain access to it.

Members of the press are specially requested to refrain from publishing the interrogatories hereafter given, so that the parties having the child in custody may not obtain the means of training him regarding his answers thereto.

On the discovery of any child, who shall be suspected of being the lost one, a photograph should be immediately obtained, if possible, and forwarded; and photographs of the parents will be sent for identification by this child.

$20,000 REWARD has been offered for the recovery of the child, and conviction of the kidnappers; all claims to which, however, will be relinquished in favor of the parties giving the information which shall lead to this result.

Abduction of Charlie [sic] *Brewster Ross.* **Broadside with albumen silver print (Philadelphia, 1874). Prints and Photographs Division, Library of Congress (LC-USZ62-121975).**

The first recorded instance of kidnapping for ransom in the United States occurred on July 1, 1874, when four-year-old Charley Brewster Ross was abducted from outside his home in the Germantown area of Philadelphia. The kidnappers demanded a $20,000 ransom. The police encouraged the family not to cooperate with the kidnappers, fearing that if they did crimes such as this would flourish. Charley Ross was never reunited with his family.

Minstrelsy was a popular form of nineteenth-century entertainment using elements of black life in song, dance, and speech. It was first performed by white actors impersonating blacks. Dan Bryant formed the Bryant's Minstrel troupe in February 1857, with the assistance of his two brothers, Jerry and Neil. They performed at their opera house in New York City, and toured the Midwest and California. The troupe was known for its sympathetic portrayal of black "plantation life," and continued performing until Dan Bryant's death in 1875.

The range of these interests is truly staggering. Aside from the obvious large categories that come readily to mind, the documentation of this collection includes such subjects as paper mills, the postal system, early music, magic, the China trade, gastronomy, etiquette, philanthropy, advertising, children's books and toys, lotteries, railroads (including train schedules and tickets), science, canals, immigration, currency (of which there is an endless supply of colonial money), bank notes, confederate money, greenbacks, federal reserve notes, etc., and a significant miscellaneous batch of materials dealing with women's history and education. In the fine arts, there are countless boxes of prints, drawings, lithographs, watercolors, photographs, and architectural designs, as well as material on music and musicians. In the practical arts one finds information about clocks, watchmakers, glassmaking, china, silk-weaving, hairdressing, sewing machines, publishing, crime, agriculture—and on and on. In entertainment, the collection abounds with items on Christmas, sports, circus, theatrical history, and games. Talk about "history from the bottom up." It is all here.

With the beginning of the nineteenth century the nation acquired a new generation of political leaders who helped usher in an exciting age that brought about a market revolution, the beginnings of an industrial society, the growth of democracy, westward expansion, and social reform. This generation of patriots instigated the War of 1812 against Great

Thomas Birch, *Perry's Victory*. Ink and wash on paper, ca. 1814. Prints and Photographs Division, Library of Congress (LC-USZC4-6663).

Master Commandant Oliver Hazard Perry's decisive victory over a desperate British fleet at the Battle of Lake Erie during the War of 1812 spurred a lively trade in images of the contest, including numerous paintings, prints, and drawings by noted Philadelphia artist Thomas Birch.

Britain in order to prove to themselves and the world that the independence of the American people had been legitimately won and that the Republic's sovereignty and rights were to be respected. One important battle of that war is beautifully depicted in a drawing by Thomas Birch. This is the Battle of Lake Erie when Commodore Oliver Hazard Perry, commanding nine vessels, engaged a British fleet outside Put-in-Bay at the western end of Lake Erie on September 10, 1813. Within three hours the larger British ships, including the flagship of the squadron, HMS *Queen Charlotte*, had been destroyed. Four others struck their colors. Two smaller British ships attempted to escape but were pursued and forced to surrender. Perry's notation on the back of a letter he wrote to General William Henry Harrison, "We have met the enemy and they are ours," helped increase his fame. The victory secured the Great Lakes for the United States and changed the balance of power in the west.

Out of that so-called "forgotten war" came a new kind of American hero who would reconstitute the shape of electoral politics. Andrew Jackson emerged from this conflict as a national icon because of his extraordinary military victory over the British at the Battle of New Orleans. Prior to his emergence on the national stage Jackson had built an impressive career for himself in Nashville and won election as major-general of the Tennessee militia. In 1813 he became embroiled in a gun fight with Thomas Hart Benton, later senator from Missouri, and his brother, Jesse. During the altercation Jesse fired two bullets and a slug straight at Jackson. His shoulder shattered by the slug and his left arm pierced by a bullet, Jackson slumped to the floor. He was carried to a room in a nearby hotel where a doctor succeeded in stanching the flow of blood. The wound was dressed with herbs and wood cuttings as prescribed by Indian lore. Exactly what the herbs and cuttings consisted of has not been generally known. But here in the Carson Collection is a rare book published in 1836 entitled *The Indian Vegetable Family Instructer* [sic] by Pierpont F. Bowker that provides one possibility. The prescription calls for the application of

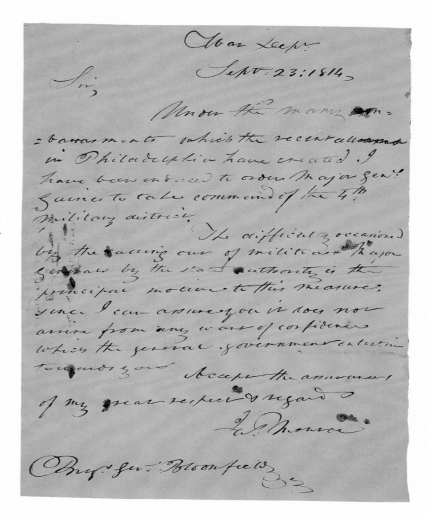

James Monroe to Brigadier General Joseph Bloomfield, War Department, September 23, 1814. Manuscript Division, Library of Congress.

In the aftermath of the August 1814 British capture of Washington and the burning of the Capitol and the President's House, Secretary of State James Monroe was also appointed acting secretary of war. In this letter to Joseph Bloomfield, former governor of New Jersey—appointed brigadier general of the U.S. Army by President James Madison in 1812, and now commander of the 3rd Military District—Monroe explained his decision to build upon American victories in the Great Lakes and at Baltimore, Maryland, by regrouping the American forces, placing Brigadier General Edmund Pendleton Gaines in command of the 4th Military District.

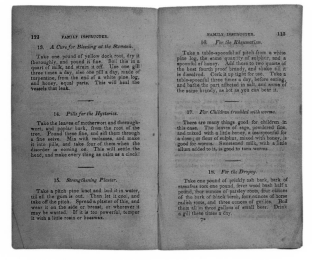

Buck's Horn, which is described as a plant of straggling branches trailing on the ground with many leaves and flowers "in small rough whitish clusters," much like a Buckshorn Plantain. It grows in barren sandy ground, says this manual. When the leaves are "bruised" and applied to a wound "of any kind" they will stop bleeding.[5] The book also provides remedies for acne and canker, stomach upset, internal bleeding, snake bite, dysentery, rheumatism, hydrophobia, dropsy, catarrh, corns, consumption, ulcers, burns, and "the falling sickness," among others.

Despite Jackson's many ailments and wounds from gunfights, his lack of credentials as a presidential candidate, and the scandals about his personal life and his "marriage" to a woman who was already married to someone else at the time, the people of the United States dismissed these impediments and elected him President in 1828 and reelected him in 1832. His inauguration outdoors and the following reception at the White House that ended in a near melee seemed to symbolize the arrival of a new era in American life and politics. The constitutions of many states had recently been amended to provide universal white manhood suffrage. Democracy had taken a significant step forward, and Jackson, the "Hero of New Orleans," symbolized what was later termed "the rise of the common man." The next several decades prior to the Civil War became known as the Age of Jackson.

It was a stupendous age in terms of social reform and innovations. There developed a powerful urge on the part of the American people to improve society and the conditions developing from an increasingly industrial and materialistic nation. Some of their efforts, such as world peace, did not get very far. Others, like abolitionism, tore the nation apart.

The Carson Collection, as one would expect, includes a great deal of material on all these reform movements: temperance, religious transformations, reforms of prisons, mental institutions, education, labor, law, and the rights of women. It is particularly full on slavery and abolition.

The introduction of slavery in the English colonies began in the seventeenth century and soon became an ongoing contest between those who strenuously objected to this "peculiar institution," as it was sometimes called, and those who contended that their economic lives depended on it. Quakers as a group were among the earliest opponents of the institution and the Carson Collection includes a great number of documents related to their efforts at emancipation. Among other things it contains the *Constitution of the Pennsylvania Society for Promoting the Abolition of Slavery and the Relief of Free Negroes Unlawfully held in Bondage*, of which Benjamin Franklin was president and Benjamin Rush and Tench Coxe secretaries. The American Colonization Society, founded in 1817 to transport freedmen to Liberia, attracted not only slaveowners to its cause but any number of philanthropic Philadelphians, and Mrs. Carson acquired a prototype of an early Liberian newspaper and a watercolor of the Liberian Senate. Furthermore, the education of African Americans is well documented in the collection and several pamphlets and flyers announce the establishment of colleges and theological seminaries for the education of black men prior to the Civil War as well as the work of the Pennsylvania Freedmen's Relief Association to educate freedmen following the war.

A. Ducîtes after A. Hervien, *The President of the United States.* **Lithograph on paper, ca. 1828. Prints and Photographs Division, Library of Congress (LC-USZC4-6670).**

During the 1820s commercial lithography developed rapidly and became recognized as a "democratic" art, which Andrew Jackson's supporters and opponents alike used to either dignify or deride his image as a simple, straightforward man of the people.

THE PRESIDENT OF THE UNITED STATES.

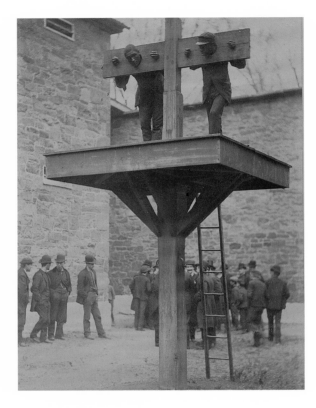

Attributed to Samuel M. Fox, *Delaware pillory and whipping post*. Albumen silver print, ca. 1889. Prints and Photographs Division, Library of Congress (LC-USZ62-121978).

Delaware's three county jail yards contained whipping posts and pillories which were used into the twentieth century. Prisoners convicted of robbery, arson, wife-beating, larceny, and other crimes publicly received five to sixty lashes to their bare backs. In 1889 a law was enacted exempting women from this form of punishment.

Some of these artifacts include musical compositions written by African Americans that describe their escape from bondage or hymns of thanksgiving on achieving their freedom. In addition to typical views of African Americans working in the fields, there is a portrait of the Jubilee Singers and a particularly gruesome photograph of a pillory in which two black men are seen in stocks. *Poems on Slavery* by Henry Wadsworth Longfellow in this collection contains such works as "The Slave's Dream," "The Slave in the Dismal Swamp," "The Slave Singing at Midnight," and "The Quadroon Girl." The first stanza of "The Slave's Dream" goes:

> *Beside the ungathered rice he lay,*
> *His sickle in his hand*
> *His breast was bare; his matted hair*
> *Was buried in the sand.*
> *Again in the midst and shadow of sleep*
> *He saw his Native Land.*

Other abolitionist poets are represented in this collection, in particular the Quaker John Greenleaf Whittier. And there are many letters about the rioting over slavery occurring in northern cities. One Quaker woman describes to her sister the anti-slavery agitation that took place in Philadelphia in 1838, a description of abolitionist meetings being held in the city, the burning of Pennsylvania Hall, and other public disturbances that occurred at the time. Race riots frequently erupted during the entire Jacksonian era.

Women played a major role in abolitionist reform, along with most of the other social reforms. But any number of them were engaged in private enterprises of various types as well. Nellie Lincoln Rossiter, for example, became a "Practical Silk Culturist" and sold silk worm eggs, mulberry trees, cuttings, and seeds for individuals to start their own silk business. Specimen boxes of cocoons with "handsome reeled silk" were sold by Rossiter for twenty-five cents each. Other women practiced "Plocacosmos" or "The Whole Art of Hair Dressing" and there were books "wherein is contained ample Rules for the Young Artizan... as well as Directions for Persons to Dress their own Hair." There are innumerable advertising covers and trade logos of business and commerce interests of both men and women in the collection.

And there are prints and photographs by the hundreds: images of men and women, including a print of the "19th wife of Brigham Young," a photo of the Indian leader and writer George Copway, and photos of churches, factories, commercial establishments, fraternal organizations, fire brigades, and street scenes.

Philadelphia was one of the leading centers for photographic experimentation in the late 1830s. Marian Carson inherited the most valuable portion of her collection of early photographs made in Philadelphia indirectly from her grandfather but added a great many more to those he left. And she was not simply interested in their uniqueness or beauty but in the historical information they provided and their relationship to written documents. Mrs. Carson was one of the first collectors who early on realized the importance of nineteenth-century documentary photography—the visual history of the country.

MRS. ANN ELIZA YOUNG,
19TH WIFE OF BRIGHAM YOUNG

Armstrong & Co. Lith. Boston, after Joseph E. Baker,
Mrs. Ann Eliza Young, 19th wife of Brigham Young.
Lithograph, n.d. Prints and Photographs Division,
Library of Congress (LC-USZC4-6668).

*Ann Eliza Young was renowned as the only one of the Mormon
leader's twenty-seven wives (she was in fact the last, not the
nineteenth as stated in the print) to sue him for divorce. Sealed
to Brigham Young in 1868 when she was a previously married
twenty-three-year-old and he was sixty-seven, she refused to
live with his other wives. Five years later, she charged him with
cruelty, neglect, and desertion and demanded exorbitant alimony.
Brigham Young was sentenced to a day in jail for refusing to
pay the court-ordered $500 a month. Ann Eliza left Utah,
published her memoirs in 1876, lectured widely to women's clubs
against the Mormon church, and married twice more.*

Unattributed, Kah-ge-ga-gah-bowh or G. Copway.
Salted-paper print with hand coloring, ca. 1860.
Prints and Photographs Division, Library of Congress
(LC-USZ62-121977).

*Kah-ge-ga-gah-bowh, or George Copway (1818–1869), was one
of the first Native Americans to have his writings published.
Copway was born in Ontario, Canada, to full-blooded Ojibway
parents, but converted to Christianity as a young boy. Among
his publications are his autobiography,* Life, Letters, and
Speeches *(1874), and* Traditional History *(1850), which
examines Ojibway life, legends, customs, language, and history.*

Tyler & Co., Foremen. Phoenix Fire Company and Mechanic Fire Company. Quarter-plate daguerreotype, ca. 1850. Prints and Photographs Division, Library of Congress (LC-USZC6-2211). Photograph by Edward Owen.

This daguerreotype was made during the golden age of volunteer firefighting when fires were fought with hand-pumped engines. The difficulty of their work is easy to overlook when viewing this portrait of firemen wearing white pants and painted hats. Dressed in their elaborate attire, fire companies were a prominent feature of parades in the nineteenth century.

Meade Brothers, Fulton Street, New York. Salted-paper print, ca. 1855. Prints and Photographs Division, Library of Congress (LC-USZ62-121979).

Lower Manhattan was the industrial and commercial center of New York City in the nineteenth century. The United States Hotel, in the center of this photograph, set the standard for New York's great hotels. Businessmen watched for incoming vessels from the promenade and observatory on the hotel's roof. The Meade brothers opened their first daguerreotype studio in Albany, New York, in the early 1840s. By 1850 the brothers had a studio on New York City's fashionable Broadway.

If photography was just beginning in the mid-nineteenth century, the art of painting reached a degree of extraordinary excellence. This occurred in part because the Jacksonian era was a romantic age that emphasized the importance of the senses and emotions in perceiving truth and beauty. Transcendentalism was its obvious expression. Its followers believed that man could "transcend" experience and reason to discover through their intuitive powers the mysteries of the universe. Man and nature were joined in what Ralph Waldo Emerson called the over-soul, and such masters as Nathaniel Hawthorne, Herman Melville, Henry Thoreau, Edgar Allen Poe, Oliver Wendell Holmes, James Russell Lowell, Walt Whitman, and others of this era frequently expressed these ideas in their written works.

Painters also absorbed this interest in nature and such excellent artists as Thomas Cole, George Inness, and Asher Brown Durant produced magnificent landscapes of some of the most impressive scenic wonders in America. Their work became known as the Hudson River school of landscape.

But there were other artists of real merit working during this period and this collection may very well reestablish the reputation of a prominent contributor to the glory of American painting who has not in the past been sufficiently appreciated or recognized.

John Rubens Smith was a master draftsman and passed along his knowledge to a generation of students. In the course of his career, Smith endeavored to record in watercolors, drawings, and prints what the United States looked like during the early National and Jacksonian periods of American history. Cities, countrysides, harbors, factories, mills, monuments, public buildings, and private homes from Boston to Charleston are captured in several hundred works contained in this collection, most of which have never been published. The watercolor paintings of the United States Capitol at the time of its rebuilding after the British had burned it during the War of 1812 are so realistic that individual details in the structure can be easily observed. These pictures can provide historians with a sense and feel of the times, with the spirit and energy of the age as major

cities arose and the nation stretched across a continent and began to evolve into an industrial society. The huge collection of Smith's works presents antebellum America in all its splendor and variety. Fortunately it has been preserved as a single unit and the public at large now can see for themselves a young republic in the throes of achieving economic and social progress just before it was rent apart by a bloody civil war.

To all intents and purposes, the Age of Jackson ended with the Mexican War in 1846. The age of reform and advancing democracy yielded to a scramble for empire and the implementation of a new ideology called Manifest Destiny. The fruits of the victory over the Mexicans brought the United States title to 500,000 square miles of territory, including what are the present states of California, Arizona, New Mexico, Nevada, Utah, a corner of Wyoming, and the western slope of Colorado. But it also brought mounting resistance by abolitionists to the expansion of slavery into these territories. Sectional rivalry and the continuing existence and likely spread of slavery inaugurated a decade of dispute in the 1850s that threatened the existence of the Union. Southerners denied that Congress could prohibit them from settling in the new territories with their human chattel. They argued that slaves were private property and property was protected under the Constitution. To outlaw slavery anywhere in the United States violated individual rights, they said, and jeopardized liberty for all. To their mind northern abolitionists threatened not only the southern way of life but the very foundation of the American system of government. The only remedy for the situation, if the demands of abolitionists triumphed, was secession, the end of the Union.

And it came with the election of Abraham Lincoln in 1860. The Carson Collection abounds in documents and pictures of the Civil War era. Such artists as William McIlvaine, Jr. and James Queen provided serene and peaceful scenes of wartime camps which can be supplemented with photographs by such masters as Mathew Brady to give a more realistic picture of the conflict. One of

James Queen (attributed) after Henry Louis Stephens (attributed), **Journey of a slave from the plantation to the battlefield.** Uncut sheet of chromolithographic cards, ca. 1863. Prints and Photographs Division, Library of Congress (LC-USZC4-6677).

In this twelve card set, the artist follows the tragic path of a slave from life on a plantation to death on a Civil War battlefield. Freed slaves were among the first black troops mustered into the Union Army, just weeks after President Lincoln read the Emancipation Proclamation in fall 1862. More than 185,000 African Americans served in the Union Army during the Civil War, and 38,000 of them, about one in five, were killed in battle.

IN THE COTTON FIELD.

THE CHRISTMAS WEEK.

THE SALE.

THE PARTING "Buy us too."

THE LASH.

BLOW FOR BLOW.

IN THE SWAMP.

FREE!

"STAND UP A MAN!"

"MAKE WAY FOR LIBERTY.!"

VICTORY!

"HE DIED FOR ME!"

the more interesting artifacts from this period is a proof sheet set of cards illustrating black history during the Civil War.

With the war's end and the victory by the North over the South the country tried to reconstruct a united nation. By 1876 all the seceded southern states had been restored to the Union. That was the year the country celebrated its Centennial and it also marks the end point of the Carsons' serious collecting interest, although there are some documents and images dealing with women's history, labor, law, medicine, architecture, politics, presidential letters, and such that extend into the twentieth century.

This vast out-reaching and in-gathering of all things American represents a stupendous achievement. This is the stuff on which revisionist history can be written. Surely the papers of the Wetherill and other Philadelphia Quaker families, the John Rubens Smith archives, and the unattributed photographs documenting American life and culture, to mention just a few possibilities, will enrich if not change our present understanding of the ever-evolving story of America.

It is to Marian S. Carson's lasting credit that she decided to keep it all together and make it available to scholars and the public in general. It is a fabulous collection, and it now belongs to the American people.

NOTES

1. Marian S. Carson, preface to William Macpherson Hornor, Jr., *Hornor Blue Book, Philadelphia Furniture* (Washington, D.C., 1977), xvii-xviii.

2. Julian P. Boyd, "A Statement of Policy by the Historical Society of Pennsylvania," *The Pennsylvania Magazine of History and Biography*, LXIV (April, 1940), 153-155.

3. Marian S. Carson, "Philadelphia A Century Ago," *The American Philatelist*, LXV (September, 1952), 909.

4. Benjamin Rush, *A Syllabus of a Course of Lectures on the Institutes of Medicine* (Philadelphia, 1795).

5. Pierpont F. Bowker, *The Indian Vegetable Family Instructer* [sic] (Boston, 1836), 20-21.

all the arrearages of interest due to the foreign officers can be p
out of it, and I suppose orders to be now on their way from
Treasury board to pay those arrearages as soon as the success of
loan shall enable it. these orders will come to their banker
Grand who alone is charged with the paiment of their debts.
I have no authority in it: but still shall be glad to be instru
-tal as far as it shall be in my power to render any service
the officers, and particularly to yourself, or any other person so
M. de Marbois honours with his friendship. I have the ho
to be with great respect Sir

Your most obedt. humble servt

Th: Jefferson

M. Sauvage. Avocat au parlement. hôtel de Malte.

Manuscript Collection

by Gerard W. Gawalt

Specialist in Early American History, Manuscript Division, Library of Congress

The Manuscript Division of the Library of Congress has been the fortunate recipient of the fruits of some of the nation's greatest individual manuscript collectors. All these gatherers of history had a focus for their collections. For Joseph Toner it was George Washington and American medicine. For Peter Force it was the American Revolution. For Edward S. Harkness and Hans P. Kraus it was early Spanish and Portuguese explorations and conquest. Individuals' accumulations of Americana, often comprising entire collections of personal papers as well as unique documents, are a vital aspect of the Library's acquisitions program.

The Marian S. Carson Collection of Americana follows in this tradition. Mrs. Carson focused on the expansion and development of America through the Centennial celebration of 1876. Her lens was Philadelphia, but her view was long and her horizon was wide. In short, she collected Americana to fit her view of America's founding and the formation of the American nation and culture—from politics to art—as seen from her vantage point on Washington Square, Philadelphia, Pennsylvania.

The Carson Collection of more than 10,000 items contains individual manuscript treasures of great rarity and value, yet its strength lies in the connections it makes in documenting the development of the United States from a bustling English colony to a burgeoning, autonomous republic. Building upon groups of materials already gathered by members of her family, Mrs. Carson created a "collection of collections." Government, politics, law, religion (particularly Free Quakers), commerce, transportation, music, education, philanthropy, medicine, postal history, women, Native Americans, and African Americans are just some of the areas of interest for this life-long collector.

Marian Carson acquired her passion for historical scholarship and many parts of her collection through family connections. From her father, Samuel S. Sadtler, a professor of chemistry at the University of Pennsylvania, and her mother Helena V. (Sachse) Sadtler, a prodigious inventor in the field of domestic arts, she undoubtedly inherited her drive and dedication to detail and knowledge. From the work of her grandfather, Julius F. Sachse, and with her husbands, William Macpherson Hornor, Jr.[1] and Joseph Carson,[2] she learned to present historical scholarship to the public and to appreciate the joys of collecting Americana.

With Philadelphia as her starting point, it is not surprising that Mrs. Carson sought the papers of the Penn family, from the founding of Pennsylvania to the family's reluctant land sales following the American Revolution. In addition to important family and provincial letters, commissions, and deeds,

Silhouette of Samuel Wetherill [Sr. or Jr.].
Manuscript Division, Library of Congress.

Samuel Wetherill, Sr. (1736-1816) was the central figure in the planning and construction of the Free Quaker Meeting House while his son and business partner Samuel Wetherill, Jr. (1764-1829) became a Pennsylvania legislator. The silhouette, of which there are many examples in the Carson Collection, was an inexpensive medium that provided one of the most realistic images of people in the late eighteenth and early nineteenth centuries, before the invention of photography. For many years, a silhouette machine was operated by an African American, Moses Williams—who also cut out the profile portraits—at Charles Willson Peale's Museum in Philadelphia.

Samuel Wetherill

Sarah Hornor, "Journal to New England," July 15, 1794.
Manuscript Division, Library of Congress.

Sarah Hornor, a young Free Quaker from Philadelphia, recorded her experiences and personal impressions during a 1794 trip from Philadelphia to visit other disavowed Quakers in New England. Suffering from ill health on and off throughout the journey, she nonetheless lived to an old age, although she never married. Her sister Amy, whom she accompanied on this journey with her husband Samuel Coates, became the mother of Dr. Benjamin H. Coates (see page 44).

Journal to New England.

7 month 15 - 1794.—

Third day morning.—

With a lassitude of mind, rather uncommon in undertakings such as this, took leave with a sigh of my Philadelphia friends, and began my journey, towards New York, in company with my brother and sister Coates, their son John, and cousin Molly Field, a sweet amiable girl, whose presance, promises a considerable addition to our satisfaction, in this long, and weary tour. I know not what could tempt me, to leave my Parents at this period of time; but their united wish, for the restoration of that health, which seems but too much on the decline; the prospect neither allures, nor interests me, tho' pictured out, in the most glowing colours of a sportive

there are original and file copies of Pennsylvania laws, petitions, and other provincial executive and legislative records. Among the hundreds of related items are a bound volume of William Penn, containing Pennsylvania laws for 1700-1709; the 1732 articles of agreement between Maryland and Pennsylvania, with related maps; and the 1698 address of the Pennsylvania Assembly to the King of Great Britain.

Important Quakers, as well as religious and educational institutions, are at the core of the collection. The papers of the Wetherill family, prosperous merchants who were known as "Fighting Quakers," or Free Quakers, because they chose to openly support the military side of the American Revolution, illustrate this aspect of the collection. As a supplier of cloth for uniforms for the Continental Army, Samuel Wetherill was considered by the Society of Friends to have broken with their pacifist convictions and was consequently disavowed by them in August 1779.[3] As merchants and manufacturers, the Wetherills became leaders in the post-war prosperity of Philadelphia and the American nation.[4] Mrs. Carson has carefully pre-

served the Wetherill family papers and added hundreds of related documents to substantiate a revisionist view of the American Revolution and the Quaker and merchant culture of Pennsylvania.

The explosive impact of the American Revolution on the nation and the Quaker community can be seen in the correspondence of the Wetherills within their extended family, as well as with prominent political leaders. Broadsides, pamphlets, legal documents, and political petitions and appeals form an integral part of the story of the Free Quakers' struggles to square their commitments to the American Revolution with their religious beliefs. An important aspect of this collection is the correspondence and travel journals produced by Free Quakers as they maintained contact with other disavowed compatriots from Dartmouth, Massachusetts, to Charleston, South Carolina.

Mrs. Carson's assembled documents related to the construction of the Free Quaker Meeting House in Philadelphia in 1783-84 include extremely rare examples of architectural drawings from this period. Samuel Wetherill, Sr. was central to the construction

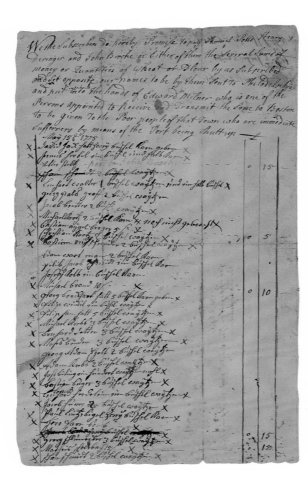

project, leading fundraising efforts, purchasing the
lot, and studying and making measurements of
several buildings before working on designs with
Revolutionary War patriot Colonel Timothy Matlack.
The architectural drawings combine with correspondence, petitions, subscription lists, broadsides,
pamphlets, accounts, and other records to reveal this
communal effort in establishing a separate Meeting,
as well as the depth of the crisis confronting the
Quaker community.[5]

Broader political aspects of the American
Revolution and the founding of America are promi-
nently represented in Marian Carson's collection. For
example, she collected a small number of symbolic
documents related to the outbreak of the Revolution
in Massachusetts, including subscription lists for
monetary support of needy Bostonians impoverished
by the forced closing of the port in 1774. Among
America's founding leaders represented here are
Thomas Jefferson, James Madison, John Hancock,
Benjamin Franklin, James Monroe, John Marshall,
Robert Morris, Charles Thomson, John Dickinson,
George Washington, Francis Hopkinson, Timothy
Pickering, Rufus King, William Paterson, and
William Shippen, Jr.

Broad strategies and specific details for financing
the war are discussed in letters and documents of
Jefferson, Morris, Pickering, Hancock, the Coates
family, and Richard Henry Lee. Notable here is
Thomas Jefferson's November 24, 1788, letter to
M. Sauvage confirming that payment will shortly be
made for the wartime services of foreign officers.
Also of note is a September 14, 1777, letter from the
Virginia delegation in Congress (including three
signers of the Declaration of Independence) to
Robert Morris asking him to safeguard funds for
them in the face of the expected evacuation of
Philadelphia.

The central role of the Continental Congress in
the founding of the nation and of Philadelphia as
its capital can be seen in the papers of Charles
Thomson, Robert Morris, Joseph Bloomfield, Jacob
Read, Robert Troup, and the Livingston and
Wetherill families. For example, there are fifteen

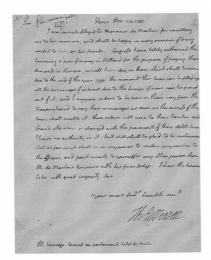

Thomas Jefferson to M. Sauvage, Paris, [France], November 24, 1788. Manuscript Division, Library of Congress.

As United States minister to France from 1785 until the outbreak of the French Revolution in 1789, Jefferson fielded many monetary claims for service in the Revolutionary War by foreign officers. In this letter, he assures M. Sauvage, an attorney to the French parliament, that these claims will be paid as soon as a loan made to the U.S. Congress by Holland has been cleared.

Benjamin Harrison, Joseph Jones, Richard Henry Lee, and Francis Lightfoot Lee to Robert Morris, Philadelphia, September 14, 1777. Manuscript Division, Library of Congress.

As a member of the Continental Congress from 1775 to 1778, Philadelphia merchant Robert Morris served on a number of committees and played a leading role in obtaining munitions and supplies and raising money to support George Washington's Continental Army. The Virginia delegates asked Morris to keep the balance of the money owed to them with the rest of the cash and effects he was moving out of Philadelphia to Lancaster, the temporary seat of government as the British and American armies engaged in battles for control of the capital at Philadelphia. Of the four signatories and the recipient of this letter, only Joseph Jones was not a signer of the Declaration of Independence.

Charles Thomson to Jacob Read, Philadelphia, July 23, 1784. Manuscript Division, Library of Congress.

Secretary of the Continental Congress Charles Thomson chastises, with gentle irony, bachelor Jacob Read, an important member from South Carolina, for tarrying among the social pleasures of Annapolis, Maryland— the American capital between 1783 and 1784—while disputes between the states are threatening the American republican confederation.

letters written by Charles Thomson, secretary of the Continental Congress, including one dated July 23, 1784, in which Thomson speaks about internal discord in the American confederation. Moreover, a December 26, 1799, letter from Secretary of State Timothy Pickering to Rufus King, United States Minister to Great Britain, announces President Washington's death and plans for an official government memorial service later that day.

Broadsides, governmental proclamations, congressional speeches, and pamphlets, some signed by notables such as Thomas Jefferson, Samuel Chase, and John Dickinson, were acquired and integrated into the collection by Mrs. Carson to complete the story of the nation's founding. These include pamphlet reports of legal cases related to the impeachment of Supreme Court justice Samuel Chase which are signed by Chase; a broadside of the Judiciary Act of March 2, 1793, assigning circuit duties to Supreme Court justices, signed by Jefferson; and a manuscript draft of William Paterson's vital speech on the separation of powers in the federal government and the necessity of the Supreme Court, delivered on July 16, 1789, during the debate on the First Judiciary Act. Letters of Samuel Wetherill, Jr., a Pennsylvania state legislator in 1800, describe the partisan efforts to choose electors for the 1800 presidential campaign between Jefferson and Adams.

Timothy Pickering to Rufus King, Department of State, December 26, 1799. Manuscript Division, Library of Congress.

Plans for the official government memorial service to honor former president George Washington later that day are described in this December 26, 1799, letter from Secretary of State Timothy Pickering to Rufus King, United States Minister to Great Britain: "A solemn procession will go from Congress Hall to one of the Churches, where an oration is to be delivered by a member of the House—General Henry Lee."

219

Nᵒ

Department of State
Dec.ʳ 26. 1799.

Dear Sir,

I inclose Five letters and one packet, addressed to Governor Davie; having reached Rhode-Island, where he & Judge Ellsworth embarked, after their departure, and with much delay been finally transmitted to this office. You will have the goodness to forward them to the Governor by a convenient opportunity, by way of Holland, Hamburg or Bremen — if a direct passage to France should be wanting.

The President, Congress, public officers, & citizens of Philadelphia, are this day to pay funeral honors to the deceased General George Washington. A solemn procession will go from Congress Hall to one of the Churches, where an oration is to be delivered by a member of the House — General Henry Lee.

I am with great respect
D.ʳ Sir your ob.ᵗ serv.ᵗ
Timothy Pickering

Rufus King Esq.ʳ Minister
Plenipotentiary &c.

Like all major collectors of Americana, Mrs. Carson was a "collector of collections," as well as items valued for their autographs. The previously described collections of the Wetherill and Penn families are just two of many such groups. Other excellent "stand alone" collections of letters, documents, journals, pamphlets, broadsides, maps, and ephemera are grouped under the Bloomfield, Stacey, Coates, Hornor, Waln, Bringhurst, Yarnall, Cresson, Clayton, Riggs, Stedman, Booth, Willing, McAllister, and, naturally, Carson families, and under Charles Thomson, Robert Troup, Stephen Girard, Robert Stewart, Elizabeth and Mary Peabody, Elizabeth Graeme Ferguson, Timothy Matlack, William Redwood, and William Rawle.[6] Although Mrs. Carson did not attempt to create a specific presidential autograph collection, she did obtain letters of at least fifteen presidents, highlighted by a longtime correspondence between Hampton L. Carson and William Howard Taft.[7] Moreover, the collection contains letters of presidents of the Continental

Congress, such as Richard Henry Lee, John Jay, John Hancock, Samuel Huntington, and Thomas Mifflin.

Not surprisingly, the Carson and Hornor families' longtime association with the legal profession led to a major collecting interest in the law.[8] Among the Supreme Court justices represented in the collection are John Marshall, John Jay, Samuel Chase, Bushrod Washington, and William Howard Taft. One of the nuggets of this collection is a group of letters, documents, pamphlets, and trial notes of William Rawle—a Quaker who was appointed United States attorney for the District of Pennsylvania in 1791 by President Washington—from the trial of Thomas Cooper, political writer and ardent supporter of Thomas Jefferson. Cooper was tried for seditious libel before Supreme Court justice Samuel Chase, sitting on circuit in April 1800, and found guilty, fined, and imprisoned. Justice Chase was strongly criticized by Republican leaders and his charges to the jury in cases such as Cooper's led to his impeachment in 1804 by the House of Representatives. None of the eight articles of impeachment received the two-thirds vote necessary for conviction in the United States Senate.[9]

American geographic and commercial expansion is vividly illustrated in Mrs. Carson's postal collection—an interest shared, if not sparked, by her husband, Joseph Carson.[10] Hundreds of postmarked letters and cards, carefully collected and arranged in special albums, illustrate the growth of America's post office, post roads, postal system, and the postal savings system. One illustrative document is an October 30, 1860, eyewitness account of one of the pony express riders departing from St. Joseph, Missouri. Although the Pony Express operated for only eighteen months in 1860 and 1861, when the telegraph and ruinous expenses put it out of business, it remains a symbol of the opening of the American West and the uniting of the East and West Coasts. Letters of postmaster generals, including Gideon Granger, Joseph Habersham, Ebenezer Hazard, Amos Kendall, John McLean, and Timothy Pickering, can also be found throughout the postal collection.

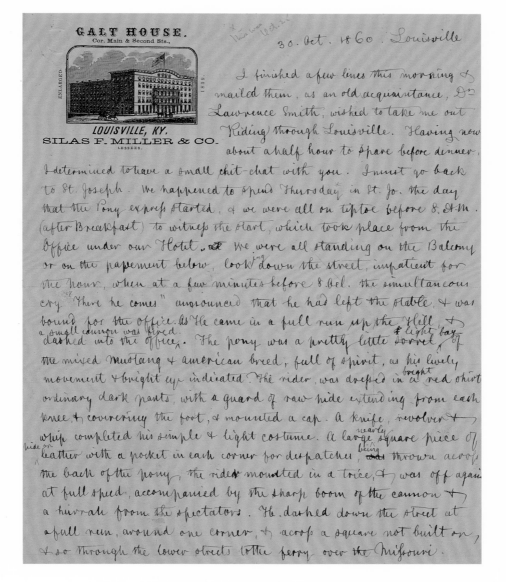

Anonymous letter from the Galt House, Louisville, Kentucky, October 30, 1860. Manuscript Division, Library of Congress.

An anonymous writer gives an eyewitness account of the excitement accompanying the early-morning departure—to the salute of a cannon and cheers of a crowd—of a Pony Express rider from St. Joseph, Missouri, en route to Sacramento, California. Just under a year later, the first telegram was transmitted to San Francisco, signalling the gradual phasing out of the short-lived but memorably picturesque relay mail service.

"…the rider mounted in a trice, and was off again at full speed accompanied by the sharp boom of the cannon & a hurrah from the spectators."

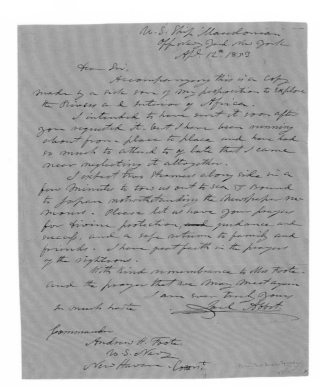

Improved transportation was a key to the central role of Philadelphia in the growth of the American nation. The role of shipping is well illustrated by letters of Robert Morris, Jean Holker, Joel Abbot, Timothy Pickering, Joshua Humphreys (shipbuilding ancestor of Joseph Carson), Henry Knox, Oliver Ellsworth, Jared Ingersoll, William H. Crawford, and the Waln, Redwood, Booth, Willing, and Coates families. Hundreds of letters, documents, broadsides, Admiralty records, and pamphlets of American naval history buttress the collection's private maritime papers. Letters of Joel Abbot and John Yarnall provide valuable information on the expansion of America's maritime presence in the Pacific. The internal transportation revolution, including steamboats, railroads, turnpikes, bridges, and canals, is yet another focal point for literally hundreds of letters, documents, and ephemera. Adams Express, Pennsylvania Railroad, Pennsylvania Canal Corporation, the Union Canal, and Schuylkill Navigation Company are among the dozens of companies represented here.

Maps and mapmaking were particularly important to a new and expanding nation. Although maps and atlases were not central to Mrs. Carson's collecting impulses, she did acquire many key maps of urban development, including two eighteenth-century pen and ink manuscript maps of Savannah. James Edward Oglethorpe, an English philanthropist and colonial adventurer, was one of the founders of Georgia's first British settlement. Mrs. Carson's maps of the "Plann of the Town of Savannah in the state of Georgia" show the growth of the settlement "on the Southern bank of the river Savannah, fifteen miles from the Sea" from 1761, when the provincial legislature approved the plan illustrated in one map, and 1796, when the city burned, as shown in the map reproduced opposite. Mrs. Carson believed that the initials "TM" on the map of the 1761 plan were those of Timothy Matlack, Philadelphia engraver of the engrossed and signed copy of the Declaration of Independence.[11]

Philadelphia was America's principal banking and commercial center during the early decades of the

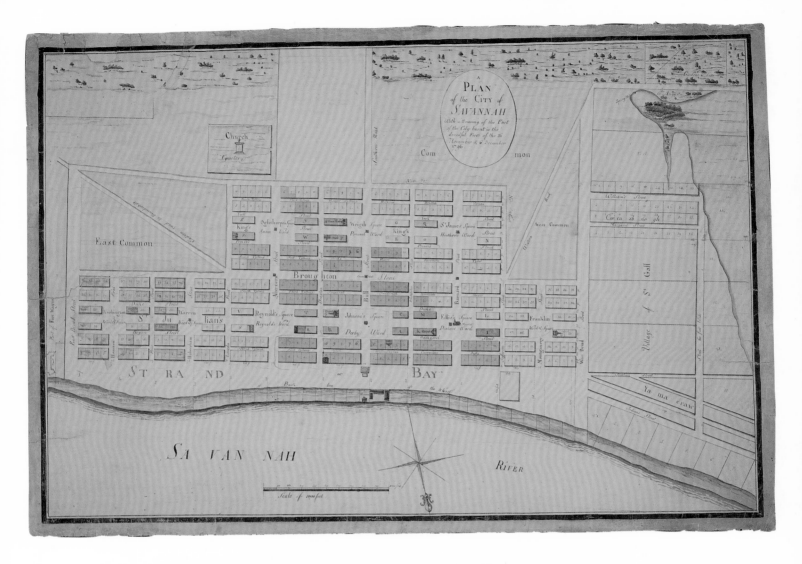

*Plan of the City of Savannah: with a drawing of a Part of the City
burnt in the dreadful Fires of 16 November & 6 December 1796.* **Pen
and ink manuscript map, ca. 1796. Geography and Map Division,
Library of Congress.**

*In 1733 James Edward Oglethorpe, an English philanthropist, led a group of
settlers to the banks of the Savannah River, creating Georgia's first settlement.
Oglethorpe planned the colonial center around several small squares, designed
to defend settlers against invasion from Native Americans and the Spanish.
Bull Street forms the central axis of the city. Incorporated as a city in 1789,
Savannah was almost destroyed by fire in 1796, as this manuscript map shows.*

American nation. Mrs. Carson represented Philadelphia's proud banking history chiefly through a collection of paper money, checks, and banknotes from national, state, and local institutions. More than one thousand lottery tickets, checks, paper monies, stocks, advertising cards, and business pictorial envelopes, arranged in large albums, are also found here. Groupings of manuscripts richly illustrate the growth of metallurgy and iron works in the Philadelphia area in the eighteenth and nineteenth centuries, as well as the production of furniture, textiles, pharmaceuticals, and paint—industries related in Pennsylvania to the Wetherill, Coates, Booth, Bringhurst, Carson, and Hornor families.[12]

Marian Carson was passionately interested in printing, publishing, and photography, particularly in Philadelphia, which, in the late eighteenth and early nineteenth centuries, was a center of American publishing. Her gathering of correspondence and documents of such printers and publishers as Robert Aitken, Benjamin Bache, Mathew Carey, William Cobbett, John Dunlap, and William Woodward supports her rare books produced by these leaders of their trade. Mrs. Carson's manuscripts on the history of photography are centered on the papers of the McAllister family, pioneers in the field in Philadelphia. However, there are only a few papers of Mrs. Carson's grandfather, Julius F. Sachse, amateur photographer and collector.

Industrial and commercial expansion could not be understood without the study of labor—free, indentured, and slave. In this section of Mrs. Carson's collection we find addresses by labor leaders and politicians, union broadsides, anti-immigrant documents, legal documents, and publications related to the trials of unionists concerned with events from Pennsylvania to California. Illustrated here is a symbolic Brotherly Union hat ribbon made for a labor organizational parade in 1823.

While most collectors have focused on the abundant materials about slavery in the South and abolition in the North, Mrs. Carson went beyond these traditional areas to acquire many letters and legal documents that reveal the life of slaves in the North—from the stark deeds of sale, to legal documents describing the behavior of slaves and their treatment, to records of manumissions and transition to freedom. A group of two dozen indentures of African Americans in the 1780s by the Philadelphia House of Employment offers a mine of information. Among these is the indenture of "Dinah, a free Negro Girl aged about twelve Years," who bound herself to servitude for sixteen years in exchange for "her manumission from Slavery." Also noteworthy is evidence of public support for slaves and freed African Americans by public officials. Especially striking is a receipt for $186, collected from members of the Pennsylvania Senate and House in

Bound indenture of Dinah, a free Negro girl, February 9, 1786. Manuscript Division, Library of Congress.

Dinah, a twelve-year-old "free Negro Girl," purchased her freedom from slavery in 1786 at the price of sixteen years of indentured servitude, according to this legal document, signed and sealed at Philadelphia in 1786.

Receipt signed by Absalom Jones, Philadelphia, December 26, 1801. Manuscript Division, Library of Congress.

Absalom Jones, minister of St. Thomas's African Episcopal Church in Philadelphia, was the recipient of money donated by members of the Pennsylvania House and Senate and presented to him by Samuel Wetherill the day after Christmas, 1801.

December 1801 for the support of Absalom Jones, minister of St. Thomas's African Episcopal Church in Philadelphia.

Philanthropy in the broadest sense of the word, as well as the Quakers' keen sense of benevolence, is encompassed by this collection. Construction of public parks, schools (public and private, for women, African Americans, and religious minorities), hospitals for the insane, welfare for the poor, public and private support for the arts and humanities, drama, and music are all themes of substantial groupings of letters, documents, broadsides, pamphlets, and related ephemera. A June 18, 1790, report of the Benjamin Franklin Bequest Committee is one of the highlights. Files on Dolley Madison, Joseph Bringhurst, sisters Elizabeth and Mary Peabody, Thomas Ford, Elizabeth Coates, the Stedman family, Quaker support records, Philadelphia corporation records and accounts, and the Philadelphia Library (Library Company of Philadelphia) include letters and documents of importance in studying the history of philanthropy.

Education of women and minorities was yet another collecting interest of Mrs. Carson. Letters of Quaker merchants James and Joseph Bringhurst help explain the creation and maintenance of a school for African Americans in Philadelphia in the 1780s. Documents related to Quaker schools abound, especially in the Wetherill and Coates family papers. Women's education is well documented in the papers of the Peabody sisters, and the Stedman, Coates, Hornor, Waln, and Wetherill families. The founding of Dickinson College and Nazareth Hall are also collection interests. Broadsides, instructional books (particularly related to penmanship, drawing, and music), and pamphlets in the Rare Book Division, as well as ephemera in the Manuscript Division bolster the information now made available to scholars.[13]

Women's occupations and avocations are key elements in Mrs. Carson's view of history. From Eliza Hornor's private accounts to Elizabeth Graeme Ferguson's fight to regain her husband's seized Loyalist property, the public and private lives of dozens of famous and anonymous women can be examined here. Records and papers of the Peabody sisters, the women of the Penn, Carson, Ferguson, Hornor, Coates, Yarnall, and Wetherill families, and records of women's clubs and women's schools (from the perspective of instructors and students) document women's work in education, public and private philanthropy, the arts, the professions, and various business endeavors. Elizabeth Peabody's March 30, 1851, letter to William Logan Fisher is illustrative of the intellectual interests of one of the leaders of the movement for the education of women.

Marian Carson's interest in collecting Americana about the decorative arts no doubt grew from her mother Helena V. Sadtler's avocation and her own research work for her collaborative work on Philadelphia furniture.[14] A life-long leader in collecting and preserving the decorative arts, she filled many albums with documents illustrating American household arts and crafts, which are of special interest to students of Americana because they provide great detail about living standards. Store and business advertising cards, found here in profusion, are among the best sources for the study of illustrative arts and life styles. There are abundant examples of marbleized paper—a classic decorative art form that became popular in the late eighteenth century—used to line drawers, shelves, book covers, ink blotters, and paper pockets for books, paper, lace, etc. Not only are

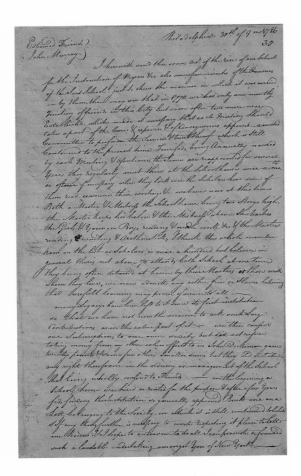

James Bringhurst to John Murray, Philadelphia, September 30, 1786. Manuscript Division, Library of Congress.

At the suggestion of the Quaker reformer Anthony Benezet, the Philadelphia Society of Friends (Quakers) established a coeducational "Negro school" in 1770. Opened to slaves and free blacks of all ages, the school offered instruction in reading, writing, arithmetic, and Christian doctrine. James Bringhurst (1730–1810), merchant and master carpenter, was among the school's trustees. and here recounts the school's history and extols the school and its students.

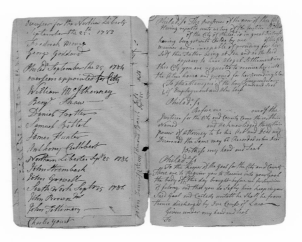

Records of the Philadelphia Overseers of the Poor, 1783-84. Manuscript Division, Library of Congress.

Philadelphia's support for the poor and sick, led by the particularly benevolent spirit of the Quakers, is illustrated by these 1783–84 records of the Overseers of the Poor for the Northern Liberties and "South Work" (Southwark).

Elizabeth Palmer Peabody to William Logan Fisher, Boston, August 1, 1851. Manuscript Division, Library of Congress.

Women's heightened involvement in America's intellectual, moral, and educational development can be seen in the career of Elizabeth Peabody, which is illustrated by her letter to William Logan Fisher, author of several works on pauperism, crime, Quakers, and the history of the Sabbath Day. At this time, Peabody, a central figure in the Boston transcendentalist movement and former publisher of The Dial, *was focusing her attention on advancing the study of history in public schools through her textbook,* Chronological History of the United States *(1856).*

these documents pleasing to the eye, but they contain vital information on product prices and availability.

Science and medicine are two fields inextricably linked in Marian Carson's collection. Again, family connections undoubtedly fostered an interest in this collecting area.[15] Medical education as well as current treatments are extremely well-documented in the papers and case books of Coates family physicians and administrators of the Pennsylvania Hospital and Asylum for the late eighteenth and early nineteenth centuries. Particularly important are the medical case books of Benjamin Hornor Coates and records and patient lists of the Pennsylvania Hospital, 1790-1840.[16] The Pennsylvania Hospital, from its founding in 1752, was the first American hospital to include treatment of the insane with the sick and physically injured. Coates was a pioneer in the use of narcotics for the treatment of the insane. Notable physicians from the Shippen and Rush families provide additional documents, correspondence, accounts, and letters. The bulk of the collection consists of a vast number of pharma-

ceutical and medical documents. One scientific paper of Benjamin H. Coates in 1843 studied the effects of "Imprisonment on Individuals of the African Variety of Mankind." Thomas Jefferson was the recipient of an 1801 report of Peter Legaux on the relationship of meteorological findings and grape production in America. Letters of noted physicians and scientists include Edward Jenner, Titian Peale, Thomas Edison, William Shippen, Jr., Benjamin Rush, Joseph Henry, and Alexander von Humboldt.

Early American music materials are highlighted (more than three hundred imprints) by Moravian and nineteenth-century specialty music, such as Civil War songs, but also include manuscript songbooks. One great rarity, however, is from an earlier period: a Francis Hopkinson manuscript songbook with several of Hopkinson's original compositions from the era of the American Revolution, which Marian Carson said she found in a consignment shop.[17] Hopkinson, lawyer, poet, essayist, and signer of the Declaration of Independence, and one of the best known American composers in the eighteenth century, wrote a celebratory song, "The Toast," to honor George Washington. "The Toast" was published in the *Pennsylvania Packet*, April 8, 1778, but this is the only known composer's copy.[18]

No collection of nineteenth-century Americana would be complete without documents related to the Civil War. Mrs. Carson has acquired materials in virtually all available formats. Again, her connection with the Hornor family benefited her collecting. Among the hundreds of representative letters and documents are a few related to Caleb W. Hornor, surgeon at the Wood Street United States Army Hospital in Philadelphia and grandfather of her first husband. Correspondence of the Clayton, Hoffman, Stacey, and Stewart families bristles with information from the warfront and the home fires. The correspondence of Robert Stewart, 72nd Pennsylvania Regiment, documents his four-year wartime service. In a July 5, 1863, letter Stewart reported to his family that he had been "wounded in the Thigh" at the Battle of Gettysburg "but it is only a Flesh Wound and I will not have to lose my Legg." Stewart's

convalescence led to a ten-day relief from duties in September, 1863 but, as can be seen in his November 11, 1863, letter, he returned to duty just in time to participate in a surprise attack on Confederate forces near Brandy Station, Virginia. The Civil War collections also include information on such well-known figures as James Buchanan, Andrew Johnson, Abraham Lincoln, David Porter, and Thaddeus Stevens, as well as maps, music, prints, and photographs.

Native Americans, particularly their relationship to expanding Anglo-American settlements, are the subjects of many documents in this collection. Materials related to the Pennsylvania Paxton Boy's attacks on "christian Indians" in 1764 and the Penn family's inter-

action with Indian tribes; a contemporary copy of Iroquois Chief Cornplanter's speech to President Washington in 1790; and John Beckley's congressional eulogy to Anthony Wayne, the victor over the Ohio tribes at "Fallen Timbers," are here. Hundreds of letters and documents centered around the Pennsylvania trading company of Slough & Gratz help to explain the course of trade and settlement in Indian lands. One unusual item is an elegy to the "Bloody Indian Battle Fought at Miami Village, November 4, 1791," printed in 1802. Missionary aid to Native Americans is well documented by items such as a 1795 report on Quaker aid to "Indian Nations" and a 1752 letter of John Brainard to Peter Livingston.

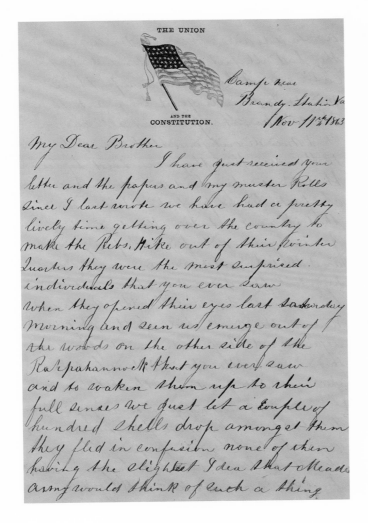

"…[the Rebs] were the most surprised individuals that you ever saw when they opened their eyes Saturday morning and seen us emerge out of the woods on the other side of the Rahpahannock [sic]… and to waken them up to their full senses we just let a couple of hundred shells drop amongst them…."

Finally, the Centennial celebration of 1876 was both a creative and collecting interest for Mrs. Carson and her family: the Centennial and the 1776 founding of the United States provide the two outside boundary markers for her collecting. Her Centennial collection is focused not only on public celebration, but on centennial efforts to improve the urban environment through cultural programs and parks, in which Julius Sachse was an active participant. Pictorial and documentary materials tracing the development of urban parks represent yet another aspect of American cultural history of keen interest to Joseph and Marian Carson.[19]

Indeed, Mrs. Carson's care and concern for the preservation of America's heritage was clearly the driving force behind her lifelong interest. Ultimately, this passion and dedication produced one of the most important manuscript collections of Americana, which is now available to all students of American history and culture in the Manuscript Division of the Library of Congress.

NOTES

1. William Macpherson Hornor, Jr. (1897-1969) married Marian Sadtler (b.1905) in 1923 . Together they compiled the *Blue Book Philadelphia Furniture* (Philadelphia, 1935; revised and reprinted, 1977). Marian Carson wrote an extended preface to the 1977 edition published by Joseph Hennage. Undoubtedly, she began acquiring much of her manuscript material related to domestic and decorative arts during the preparation of this work. Many of the same families, such as Waln, Coates, Yarnall, Carson, Hornor, Bringhurst, and Macpherson, appear in this book, Marian's family tree, and her manuscript collection.

2. Joseph Carson (1883-1953) married Marian Sadtler Hornor in 1942, several years after her divorce from William Macpherson Hornor, Jr. Carson, a lawyer and civic leader, was an avid collector of postal history, part of which remains in Marian Carson's collection. Director of the Fairmount Park Commission, president of the Free Library of Philadelphia, trustee of the Philadelphia Museum

of Art, and vice president of the Historical Society of Pennsylvania were just some of the positions of civic leadership held by Joseph Carson.

3. Samuel Wetherill, Sr. established the Religious Society of Friends, or Free Quakers, with a number of other prominent Philadelphians who had also been disowned for their participation in the Revolutionary War, including Col. Timothy Matlack, White Matlack, Col. Clement Biddle, Owen Biddle, Benjamin Say, Christopher Marshall, Joseph Warner, and Moses Bartram. See John W. Jordan, ed., *Colonial Families of Philadelphia* (New York, 1911), II, 994.

4. After the war, Samuel and his namesake pioneered in the production of white lead paint in America. See Mrs. S. P. Wetherill, *Samuel Wetherill and the Early Paint Industry of Philadelphia* (City History Society of Philadelphia, 1916).

5. As Samuel Wetherill, Sr. was the central figure in the construction of the Free Quaker Meeting House, as well as first clerk and preacher of the Society, his descendant Samuel Price Wetherill was clerk of the Society of Free Quakers in 1957, the year that the building was acquired by the Commonwealth of Pennsylvania in executing the Independence Mall project. Marian Carson had acquired the Wetherill papers and broadsides privately from a member of the family. Her knowledge of the Wetherills and the Free Quakers had become so detailed that she was retained as a historical advisor by the Society of Free Quakers that year as it planned to move and restore its former Meeting House at Fifth and Arch Streets: in June 1961, the building was moved 33 feet west and 8 feet south to allow for the widening of Fifth Street, but without the original cellars and vaults designed by Timothy Matlack, which were left behind in the bed of the widened street. Utilizing the Wetherill Papers, Marian Carson was able to locate original sections of the building and provide valuable information on the construction, including original architectural drawings and lists of building supplies (Hugh Scott, "History on the Mall: Free Quakers' Meeting House at Fifth and Arch to be moved and restored," *The Philadelphia Inquirer Magazine*, December 29, 1957). Architect Charles E. Peterson was not given access to the Wetherill family papers by Mrs. Carson when he prepared his *Notes on the Free Quaker Meeting House* in 1966 for the architectural firm commissioned by the Commonwealth of Pennsylvania to restore the building at its new location. However, he cited Mrs. Carson's undated typescript paper, "The Society of Free Quakers of the Revolution," which provided some of the information in his report.

6. Many of these collections are indeed family collections in the truest sense, because Marian Carson was connected through blood and marriage to at least the Macpherson, Hornor, Coates, Hollingsworth, Humphreys, Yarnall, and Carson families.

7. William Macpherson Hornor, Jr., Joseph Carson, and his father, Hampton L. Carson, were autograph collectors.

8. Joseph and his father, Hampton L. Carson, were graduates of the law school at the University of Pennsylvania. Hampton, professor of law and attorney general of Pennsylvania, wrote books on the United States Supreme Court and the United States Constitution. William M. Hornor, father of Marian's first husband, was also a graduate of the law school at the University of Pennsylvania and a founder of the Society of Colonial Wars in Pennsylvania.

9. Also found here are the Philadelphia Law Society records, 1780s; Samuel Harvey's accounts as treasurer of the Philadelphia Guardians of the Poor, 1806-1811; Garret Wall's Record of Attorneys in Philadelphia, 1709-1804; and a Pennsylvania Common Pleas case book, 1798.

10. Joseph Carson assembled an extremely large and important collection of American stampless covers, but only a fragment remains in the Carson Collection.

11. Atlases and maps, such as the two Savannah maps, which are not integral to the manuscript holdings, will be assigned to the Geography and Map Division of the Library of Congress.

12. See Mrs. S. P. Wetherill's previously cited paper on Samuel Wetherill and the lead paint industry, and Marian Carson and William Macpherson Hornor, Jr.'s book on Philadelphia furniture. Business accounts include Richard Waln's daybook, 1768-69; Benjamin Shoemaker's corporation accounts, 1745-1771; David Dishler's receipt book, 1772-1796; White Lead Manufactory, 1804; and Dolley Madison's first husband John Todd, Jr.'s receipt book, 1786-1791.

13. Members of Marian Carson's extended family have played key roles in educational and civic institutions in Pennsylvania for generations. For example, her father, Samuel S. Sadtler, and her grandfather, Samuel P. Sadtler, were professors at the University of Pennsylvania. Her husband, Joseph Carson, held many civic service positions, including president of the Fairmount Park Commission.

14. Marian Carson was a founding member of The Decorative Arts Trust of Philadelphia and served as its vice president. Her mother, Helena V. (Sachse) Sadtler (1873-1956) was a skilled inventor of decorative and domestic arts and registered a large number of patents on her inventions and technical developments. See also previous citations to Marian S. Carson's work on the *Blue Book Philadelphia Furniture*.

15. Mrs. Carson's first husband, William Macpherson Hornor, Jr., had ties to the Coates family; his grandfather, Caleb Wright Hornor, was a surgeon and hospital administrator during the Civil War; and her second spouse, Joseph Carson, was descended from Dr. Joseph Carson (1808-1876), a physician/professor in Philadelphia and the author of several books on medical history and medical botany.

16. Marian Carson used these Coates records and other manuscripts from her collection in writing "Benjamin Hornor Coates, M.D. (1797-1881): A Study Based on His Manuscripts," *Transactions & Studies of the College of Physicians of Philadelphia*, 4th ser., 35 (October, 1967), 63-68, and in exhibits in Philadelphia and New York. Coates's father, Samuel, was a longtime administrator of the Pennsylvania Hospital.

17. Marian S. Carson said in a September 16, 1996, taped interview at the Library of Congress that she had found it in a consignment shop in Paoli, Pennsylvania, where it had been left by a descendant of Hopkinson.

18. Manuscript and printed music not integral to the basic manuscript collection will be housed in the Rare Book and Special Collections Division and the Music Division of the Library of Congress.

19. Joseph Carson's role with the Fairmount Park Commission and Julius Sachse's interest in the United States Centennial Exposition no doubt influenced Mrs. Carson's collecting interests.

A DIAMOND BREASTPI[N]

CHARITY.

Adorn your bosom with this precious Pin;

It shines without, and warms the heart withi[n]

Rare Printed Material

by Rosemary Fry Plakas

American History Specialist, Rare Book and Special Collections Division, Library of Congress

Tucked in amongst the treasured tomes of the Marian S. Carson book collection is a charming little piece on conduct, dressed in a ruby red cover trimmed in gold. Each page of Hannah Lindley Murray's *The American Toilet* (New York, 1827) pictures a dressing-table item, carefully hand-colored, with a hinged flap covering the name of a virtue described in the accompanying poem. This tiny gem not only celebrates qualities like perseverance, benevolence, and good humor that are reflected in Mrs. Carson's life, but it combines several themes—education, women, early American printing, and the decorative arts—that have brought her delight and influenced her collecting pursuits.

In addition to forming a significant collection of children's books and games, Marian Carson amassed an amazing array of books, pamphlets, broadsides, and printed ephemera to support and enrich her collection in other formats. Fortunately for the Library, her interests in early American printing, the formative years of the American Republic, nineteenth-century social history, culinary arts, and children's literature parallel some of the Rare Book and Special Collections Division's major strengths and yet bring an impressive number of new titles to the Library's collections. Mrs. Carson's ability to seek out unique treasures and to accumulate complementary materials on such a wide range of subjects is truly admirable.

Marian Carson's efforts to continue acquiring in an area of special significance to her grandfather, Julius F. Sachse, are reflected by a number of works in her collection related to early Pennsylvania German history and culture. From 1890 until his death in 1919, Sachse devoted much of his efforts to exploring the history of German pietist sects that emigrated to Pennsylvania during the late seventeenth century in search of religious freedom. Many of his writings focus on the fraternity of mystics led by Johannes Kelpius, which established its hermitage in 1694 near Germantown on a wilderness ridge overlooking Wissahickon Creek, and its virtual successor, the more enduring communal experiment founded by the charismatic Sabbatarian Conrad Beissel at Ephrata in 1732. Although Sachse gave most of the rare documents and books he collected about these sects to the Seventh Day Baptist Historical Society, a small number of some of the rarest and perhaps most treasured items remained with the Sachse family and eventually were given to Marian Carson by her aunt.

In an effort to promote the spiritual welfare of his German neighbors and to prepare himself and his followers for the Second Coming of Christ, Johannes Kelpius published around 1700 a small devotional pamphlet, *Kurtzer Begriff oder leichtes Mittel zu beten*, describing how spiritual serenity could be achieved through inward prayer and physical isolation. There is no known extant copy of this, the first German

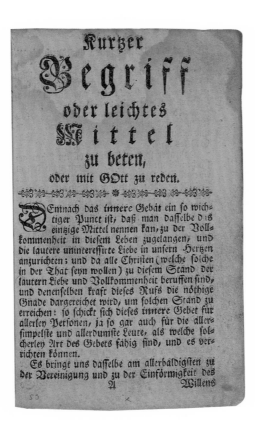

devotional book printed in America. The only known copy of the second German edition of 1756 is the Sachse copy which is now a part of the Carson Collection at the Library of Congress. While Sachse attributed the printing of this edition to Benjamin Franklin and Anthony Armbruster, recent scholarship suggests that the border ornaments and tailpiece design point to the Christopher Saur press in Germantown.[1] Kelpius's authorship is authenticated in a manuscript note by Christian Lehman on the only known copy (Historical Society of Pennsylvania) of the 1761 English translation that also identifies Lehman's teacher, the English physician Christopher Witt, as translator.[2]

The earliest work published by Conrad Beissel in Pennsylvania, *Mystyrion Anomias*, was a 1728 treatise advocating the seventh day as the true Sabbath by holy command of God. Although this tract had great influence on Sabbath observation among rural German communities, no copy of the original German edition is known to be extant. Sachse found his copy of the rare 1729 first English translation, *Mystyrion Anomias the Mystery of Lawlesness* [sic], bound with British tracts about the Sabbath in a volume formerly owned by Henry Gurney of Philadelphia.[3]

Considering the essential role music played in the worship of all German religious sects, it is not surprising that many of their early printed works were hymnals. Beissel is best known as a prolific hymn writer, his first compilation of sixty-five hymns being published in 1730. During his solitary retreat on Cocalico Creek, just prior to forming the Ephrata Society, Beissel perfected and enlarged his hymnal, composing two dozen new songs and including several by other brethren.[4] This rare second compilation of German hymns, published in 1732 by Benjamin Franklin, offers a "Prelude to the New World…

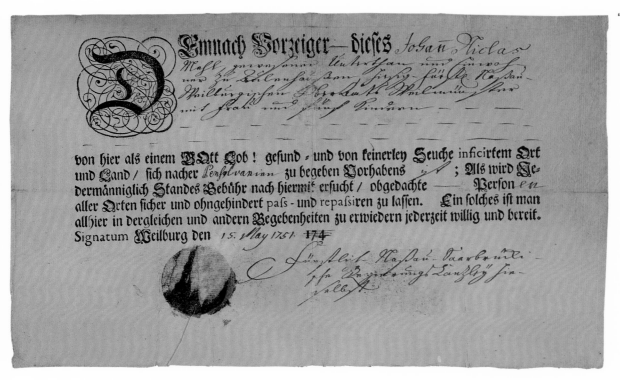

**"Demnach Vorzeiger"
(German health
certificate). Manuscript
entry on printed form,
Weilburg, May 15, 1751.
Rare Book and Special
Collections Division,
Library of Congress.**

*German immigration to
Pennsylvania grew steadily
throughout the middle decades
of the eighteenth century.
This document certifyng that
the family of Johan Niclas
Mase was free of disease
at embarkation, was no
insurance against the health
hazards of the ocean voyage.
Overcrowding, poor nutrition,
and unsanitary conditions
aboard ship brought illness or
death to many immigrants,
especially children.*

illustrated in songs of Love, Praise, Suffering, Power and Experience." In addition to being a rare Franklin printing, known only in ten copies, the Carson copy is one of only two copies that contains a fourteen-line paste-in used to correct the third stanza of hymn 86, page 141.[5] Other German items include a German health certificate, dated Weilburg, May 1751, permitting travel to Pennsylvania; several German primers; almanacs, popular medical manuals, and veterinary guides from the Saur press; and early-nineteenth-century Baptist sermons and treatises.

Carson's interest in early German printing is only part of a much broader interest in early American printing in general, demonstrated by her acquiring nearly five hundred works printed before 1801. Philadelphia printing is a special focus, the collection having at least one example from many of the early Philadelphia printers. America's best known colonial printer, Benjamin Franklin, is represented here by at least seven items from his press, as well as another ten by or about him. Franklin's personal favorite from his press is *M. T. Cicero's Cato Major, or his Discourse of Old-Age*, published in Philadelphia in 1744. Considered to be the pinnacle of fine printing in Colonial America, this piece was printed in one thousand copies, with title page in red and black and in Caslon type large enough to accommodate those with failing eyesight.[6]

Although the Library's holdings of early American imprints include nearly half of all known titles printed here before 1801, the Carson Collection brings a significant number of new ones, including *The Universal Peace-maker… by Philanthropos*, printed by Anthony Armbruster in 1764; John Searson's 1770 sermon *Two Discourses Delivered in the Prison of Philadelphia*; David Garrick's play *The Irish Widow*, 1773; Samuel Jackson's *Emma Corbett: Exhibiting Henry and Emma, the Faithful Modern Lovers*, 1783;

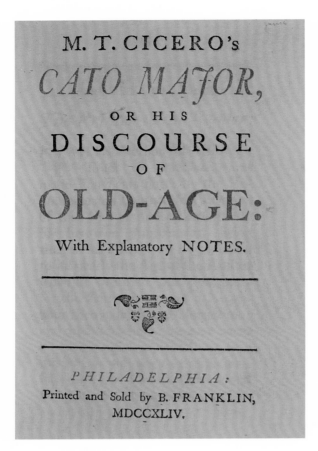

M. T. CICERO's

CATO MAJOR,

OR HIS

DISCOURSE

OF

OLD-AGE:

With Explanatory NOTES.

PHILADELPHIA:
Printed and Sold by B. FRANKLIN,
MDCCXLIV.

early session laws of Pennsylvania, 1744-1752, and a 1764 act "for preventing tumults and riotous assemblies." Two 1770 Susquehannah Company pamphlets, extensively annotated by Ezra Stiles, discuss Connecticut's land claims in Pennsylvania's Wyoming Valley. Polemics from both sides of the propaganda war that prepared the colonies for armed rebellion are numerous, including John Hancock's 1774 oration on the Boston massacre and Granville Sharp's *Declaration of the People's Natural Right to a Share in the Legislature* (New York, 1774). Early volumes of the *Journal of the Proceedings of the* [Continental] *Congress* include copies originally owned by delegates Benjamin Franklin, Oliver Ellsworth, and John Dickinson.

Marian Carson's passion for pursuing entire collections and large lots has been demonstrated elsewhere; however, she made equal effort to seek those special solitaires that add stunning brilliance to her collection. In July 1948, while waiting at their summer house in the Catskills for a ship to arrive in New York with an English nanny for their four-year-old daughter and another baby expected soon, the Carsons stopped off at an estate sale at an old Dutch farmhouse on the Hudson River near Kingston, New York, the home for nearly two and a half centuries of the Dederick family. In trunks in the attic, they found, among other things, medical paraphernalia belonging to a doctor in the 1790s and an extremely rare copy of one of the earliest broadside editions of the Declaration of Independence, sometimes attributed to the New York printer Samuel Loudon.[7]

Other Revolutionary War era broadsides in Mrs. Carson's collection were printed in Philadelphia, including proclamations by General Howe during the British occupation of Philadelphia (1777), remonstrances by Quakers (1777), and resolves of Congress for regulating the clothing department (1779), reorganizing the inspector's department (1782), and urging states to meet their quotas for financing the war (1785). Particularly fascinating is the rare folio broadside announcing the order of procession for the July 4, 1788, celebration honoring the establishment of the Constitution, ordered by Francis Hopkinson, chairman of arrangements.

and Mathew Carey's *A Plum Pudding for the Humane, Chaste, Valiant, Enlightened Peter Porcupine*, 1799—all published in Philadelphia.

Even where the Library already possesses copies, a good number of Marian Carson's books have special inscriptions, annotations, or association interest. For instance, the autograph signature of John McKinly, assembly delegate and, later, first revolutionary governor of Delaware, appears on the title page of *Aitken's General Register, and the Gentleman's and Tradesman's Complete Annual Account Book, and Calendar, For… 1773* (Philadelphia, 1772) and the "Almanac" portion contains extensive manuscript notes by McKinly recording the weather.

Carson's interest in political history, and particularly the formative years of our nation, is illustrated by an array of material, beginning with compilations of

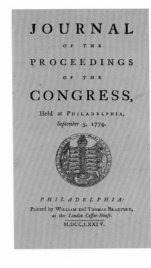

TO THE

INHABITANTS OF THE BRITISH COLONIES IN NORTH AMERICA.

AS the following GENERAL REGISTER is the firſt attempt of the kind that hath yet appeared in theſe colonies, the publiſher begs leave to beſpeak the patronage and encouragement of all thoſe who are friends to the political and commercial intereſts of BRITISH AMERICA.

The utility of ſuch a work hath been long experienced and acknowledged in the Mother Country : And the time is now come, when it muſt be equally neceſſary and advantageous here. The intercourſe and connection of the ſeveral colonies with each other, is enlarging and growing ſtronger every day ; ſo that it becomes a matter of ſome conſequence to every inhabitant, to be acquainted with the *public offices* and *officers*, not only of the particular province in which he reſides, but in all the other provinces on the continent. Buſineſs will make ſuch a manual as this abſolutely neceſſary to ſome ; and *curioſity* at leaſt may hereby be agreeably ſatisfied in others. To *ſtrangers* too it muſt be particularly beneficial ; as they may juſtly be ſuppoſed to be much leſs acquainted with theſe matters than thoſe who continually reſide amongſt us.

The undertaking hath already been much approved of and countenanced by many ingenious men and very competent judges in this and the neighbouring provinces. To theſe gentlemen the publiſher moſt gratefully acknowledges his obligations for the materials with which they have chearfully furniſhed him. The greater part of theſe materials may be depended upon for their authenticity, as they are taken from the original books of records in the ſeveral provinces.

Many errors and deficiencies, perhaps, will be found in this *firſt* publication. Theſe however, the publiſher flatters himſelf will be kindly pointed out to him, and ſuch pieces of intelligence communicated, as will enable him to execute his deſign more fully and accurately in the next year's regiſter.

ROBERT AITKEN.

Philadelphia, 16 Dec. 1772.

In CONGRESS, July 4, 1776.

A DECLARATION

By the REPRESENTATIVES of the

UNITED STATES OF AMERICA,

In GENERAL CONGRESS Assembled.

WHEN in the Courfe of human Events, it becomes neceffary for one People to diffolve the political Bands which have connected them with another, and to affume among the Powers of the Earth, the feparate and equal Station to which the Laws of Nature and of Nature's God entitle them, a decent Refpect to the Opinions of Mankind requires that they fhould declare the Caufes which impel them to the Separation.

We hold thefe Truths to be felf-evident, that all Men are created equal, that they are endowed by their Creator with certain unalienable Rights, that among thefe are Life, Liberty and the Purfuit of Happinefs.—That to fecure thefe Rights, Governments are inftituted among Men, deriving their juft Powers from the Confent of the governed, that whenever any Form of Government becomes deftructive of thefe Ends, it is the Right of the People to alter or to abolifh it, and to inftitute new Government, laying its Foundation on fuch Principles, and organizing its Powers in fuch Form, as to them fhall feem moft likely to effect their Safety and Happinefs. Prudence, indeed, will dictate that Governments long eftablifhed fhould not be changed for light and tranfient Caufes; and accordingly all Experience hath fhewn, that Mankind are more difpofed to fuffer, while Evils are fufferable, than to right themfelves by abolifhing the Forms to which they are accuftomed. But when a long Train of Abufes and Ufurpations, purfuing invariably the fame Object, evinces a Defign to reduce them under abfolute Defpotifm, it is their Right, it is their Duty, to throw off fuch Government, and to provide new Guards for their future Security. Such has been the patient Sufferance of thefe Colonies; and fuch is now the Neceffity which conftrains them to alter their former Syftems of Government. The Hiftory of the prefent King of Great-Britain is a Hiftory of repeated Injuries and Ufurpations, all having in direct Object the Eftablifhment of an abfolute Tyranny over thefe States. To prove this, let Facts be fubmitted to a candid World.

He has refufed his Affent to Laws, the moft wholefome and neceffary for the public Good.

He has forbidden his Governors to pafs Laws of immediate and preffing Importance, unlefs fufpended in their Operation till his Affent fhould be obtained; and when fo fufpended, he has utterly neglected to attend to them.

He has refufed to pafs other Laws for the Accommodation of large Diftricts of People, unlefs thofe People would relinquifh the Right of Reprefentation in the Legiflature, a Right ineftimable to them, and formidable to Tyrants only.

He has called together legiflative Bodies at Places unufual, uncomfortable, and diftant from the Depofitory of their public Records, for the fole Purpofe of fatiguing them into Compliance with his Meafures.

He has diffolved Reprefentative Houfes repeatedly, for oppofing with manly Firmnefs his Invafions on the Rights of the People.

He has refufed for a long Time, after fuch Diffolutions, to caufe others to be elected; whereby the legiflative Powers, incapable of Annihilation, have returned to the People at large for their exercife; the State remaining in the mean Time expofed to all the Dangers of Invafion from without, and Convulfions within.

He has endeavoured to prevent the Population of thefe States; for that Purpofe obftructing the Laws for Naturalization of Foreigners; refufing to pafs others to encourage their Migrations hither, and raifing the Conditions of new Appropriations of Lands.

He has obftructed the Adminiftration of Juftice, by refufing his Affent to Laws for eftablifhing judiciary Powers.

He has made Judges dependent on his Will alone, for the Tenure of their Offices, and the Amount and Payment of their Salaries.

He has erected a Multitude of new Offices, and fent hither Swarms of Officers to harrafs our People, and eat out their Subftance.

He has kept among us, in Times of Peace, Standing Armies, without the Confent of our Legiflatures.

He has affected to render the Military independent of and fuperior to the Civil Power.

He has combined with others to fubject us to a Jurifdiction foreign to our Conftitution, and unacknowledged by our Laws; giving his Affent to their Acts of pretended Legiflation:

For quartering large Bodies of armed Troops among us:

For protecting them, by a mock Trial, from Punifhment for any Murders which they fhould commit on the Inhabitants of thefe States:

For cutting off our Trade with all Parts of the World:

For impofing Taxes on us without our Confent:

For depriving us, in many Cafes, of the Benefits of Trial by Jury:

For tranfporting us beyond Seas to be tried for pretended Offences:

For abolifhing the free Syftem of Englifh Laws in a neighbouring Province, eftablifhing therein an arbitrary Government, and enlarging its Boundaries, fo as to render it at once an Example and fit Inftrument for introducing the fame abfolute Rule into thefe Colonies:

For taking away our Charters, abolifhing our moft valuable Laws, and altering fundamentally the Forms of our Governments:

For fufpending our own Legiflatures, and declaring themfelves invefted with Power to legiflate for us in all Cafes whatfoever.

He has abdicated Government here, by declaring us out of his Protection and waging War againft us.

He has plundered our Seas, ravaged our Coafts, burnt our Towns, and deftroyed the Lives of our People.

He is, at this Time, tranfporting large Armies of foreign Mercenaries to compleat the Work of Death, Defolation and Tyranny, already begun with Circumftances of Cruelty and Perfidy, fcarcely parallelled in the moft barbarous Ages, and totally unworthy the Head of a civilized Nation.

He has conftrained our fellow Citizens taken Captive on the high Seas to bear Arms againft their Country, to become the Executioners of their Friends and Brethren, or to fall themfelves by their Hands.

He has excited domeftic Infurrections amongft us, and has endeavoured to bring on the Inhabitants of our Frontiers, the mercilefs Indian Savages, whofe known Rule of Warfare, is an undiftinguifhed Deftruction of all Ages, Sexes and Conditions.

In every Stage of thefe Oppreffions we have petitioned for Redrefs, in the moft humble Terms: Our repeated Petitions have been anfwered only by repeated Injury. A Prince, whofe Character is thus marked by every Act which may define a Tyrant, is unfit to be the Ruler of a free People.

Nor have we been wanting in Attentions to our Britifh Brethren. We have warned them from Time to Time of Attempts by their Legiflature to extend an unwarrantable Jurifdiction over us. We have reminded them of the Circumftances of our Emigration and Settlement here. We have appealed to their native Juftice and Magnanimity, and we have conjured them by the Ties of our common Kindred to difavow thefe Ufurpations, which would inevitably interrupt our Connections and Correfpondence. They too have been deaf to the Voice of Juftice and of Confanguinity. We muft, therefore, acquiefce in the Neceffity, which denounces our Separation, and hold them, as we hold the reft of Mankind, Enemies in War, in Peace, Friends.

We, therefore, the Reprefentatives of the UNITED STATES OF AMERICA, in General Congrefs affembled, appealing to the Supreme Judge of the World for the Rectitude of our Intentions, do, in the Name and by the Authority of the good People of thefe Colonies, folemnly Publifh and Declare, That thefe United Colonies are, and of Right ought to be, FREE AND INDEPENDENT STATES; that they are abfolved from all Allegiance to the Britifh Crown, and that all political Connection between them and the State of Great-Britain, is and ought to be totally diffolved; and that as FREE AND INDEPENDENT STATES, they have full Power to levy War, conclude Peace, contract Alliances, eftablifh Commerce, and to do all other Acts and Things which INDEPENDENT STATES may of Right do. And for the Support of this Declaration, with a firm Reliance on the Protection of Divine Providence we mutually pledge to each other our Lives, our Fortunes, and our facred Honour.

Signed by ORDER and in BEHALF of the CONGRESS,

JOHN HANCOCK, Prefident.

ATTEST.

CHARLES THOMSON, SECRETARY.

Although Carson's focus on the Free or Fighting Quakers is well documented, her book collection also includes twenty works related to the traditional Quakers, or Society of Friends, mostly doctrinal treatises published before 1800. Titles new to the Library include John Perrot's treatise on salvation, *Beames of Eternal Brightness* (London, 1661), and Joseph Pike's *Epistle to the National Meeting of Friends in Dublin* (Philadelphia, 1770). A 1778 collection of Quaker religious tracts given by Anthony Benezet to Mary Norris Dickinson, the Quaker wife of John Dickinson, is heavily annotated.

One of the ironies of the American revolutionary struggle is the patriots' harsh treatment of those who did not actively support their cause, particularly in moderate Pennsylvania. Because of their traditional pacifist beliefs, Quakers were ordered by their leaders to maintain strict neutrality, to refuse to serve in combat or to pay taxes for the war effort, and to take no oaths of loyalty to either side. When word of Howe's advance towards Philadelphia arrived in late August 1777, shortly after intelligence that seemed to implicate Quakers in passing military information to the British, Congress quickly recommended that the Pennsylvania Executive Council confine any persons suspected of threatening the public safety. The state council immediately arrested twenty-six men, mostly Quakers, who had refused to take loyalty oaths and confined them in the Mason's Lodge without a hearing. In their *Address to the Inhabitants of Pennsylvania* (Philadelphia, 1777), Israel Pemberton, John Hunt, Samuel Pleasants, Henry Drinker, Thomas Wharton, and seventeen others claimed their rights as freemen against arbitrary confinement and requested a hearing to vindicate their characters.[8]

Marian Carson, however, did not confine her collecting of early American religious publications to works by German pietists and Quakers. In ecumenical fashion, she also acquired catechisms, doctrinal treatises, mission reports, and sermons produced by Anglicans, Catholics, Episcopalians, Lutherans, Methodists, Methodist Episcopalians, Moravians, Presbyterians, and Protestant Episcopalians, as well as works by Emanuel Swedenborg and Henri Godineau. At least twenty are titles not previously held by the Library, including Cambridge professor Richard Watson's *Apology for the Bible: in a Series of Letters Addressed to Thomas Paine* (Philadelphia, 1796). The collection adds a second copy of the rare Aitken Bible, the first complete Bible printed in English in the United States and recommended by Congress in 1782, as well as publisher William Young's 1802 Bible,

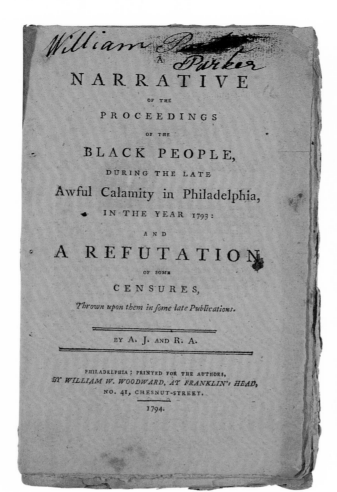

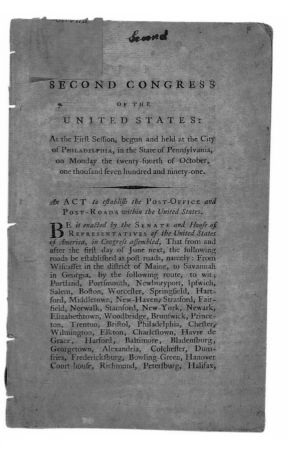

These two documents represent important threads in the rich tapestry of Mrs. Carson's collecting interests: African American and medical history and the innovative work of the early federal congresses to create the foundations of the new national government.

bound with the *Psalms of David in Metre* (Philadelphia, 1805), which Young gave to his granddaughter Sarah A. McAllister in 1829.

Mrs. Carson's pursuit of political history brings together significant material that demonstrates the innovative work of the early federal congresses to create the foundations of the new national government. Nearly sixty documents and broadsides include committee reports, bills, and rare separate printings of acts to establish the judicial courts, the mint, and the post office and post roads. Postal history, a favorite subject of Joseph Carson, is documented with a number of items covering changes in postal regulations, the Sunday mail controversy, and various trials of mail robbers.

Although Marian Carson amassed a considerable collection of political publications, she became increasingly absorbed in securing evidence of America's social, cultural, and economic history. For example, her documentation of the rise of American manufacturing brings several new titles to the Library, including memorials from merchants and farmers supporting duties on imported goods, the 1804 *Plan* and the 1820 *Memorial* of the Pennsylvania Society for the Encouragement of American Manufactures, of which Samuel Wetherill, Jr. was a manager, and pamphlets featuring various industries, such as the 1890s' *History of the Hat Trimming Controversy*. A significant collection of trade catalogs, many with generous illustrations, offer another window on nineteenth-century American manufacturing, ranging from textile machinery to theatrical wigs.[9]

Two of Mrs. Carson's collecting interests, African Americans and medical history, were combined in her study of the involvement of Philadelphia's then small black community in the catastrophic yellow fever epidemic which struck the city in August 1793, killing four thousand people, nearly ten percent of the residents.[10] Young and old, rich and poor succumbed to the scourge, which stifled both business and government. At Dr. Benjamin Rush's request, Absalom Jones and Richard Allen, free black ministers and leaders of the African Society, organized their people

to care for the sick and bury the dead. Despite the heroic efforts of many blacks, publisher Mathew Carey, in his tracts on the fever, charged some blacks with plundering homes and demanding exorbitant fees for their services. To set the record straight, Allen and Jones produced *A Narrative of the Proceedings of the Black People* (Philadelphia, 1794), describing scenes they had witnessed while attending thousands of sick and dying that did not reflect well on the behavior of many whites. Carson has collected two dozen pamphlets on yellow fever in Philadelphia, as well as another dozen on other medical topics. Titles new to the Library include *Every Man his own Physician* (Philadelphia, 1794); *Afflicted Man's Companion* (Wilmington, Delaware, 1796); Dr. Benjamin Rush's *Syllabus of a Course of Lectures on the Institutes of Medicine* (Philadelphia, 1795); and Pierpoint Bowker's *Indian Vegetable Family Instructer* [sic] (Boston, 1836) (see page 18).

In addition to the biography of Richard Allen and the history of the African Methodist Episcopal Church, Mrs. Carson acquired treatises on slavery by Anthony Benezet and Thomas Clarkson, memorials of early abolition societies, and reports of the American Colonization Society's efforts to send free blacks to Liberia. Of special note is the 1826 prospectus for the *Liberia Herald*. Expectations for establishing the first Liberian newspaper were dashed when the printer, Charles Force, died of the fever shortly after arriving in Monrovia.[11]

Once again, Mrs Carson linked two of her favorite topics, women and education, in a number of significant books in her collection, including several textbooks written specifically for young ladies and reports on girls' schools. One of the most engaging authors is Quaker Milcah Martha Hill Moore (1740-1829) who, at twelve, upon the death of her mother, left the Madeira island home of her transplanted Marylander parents and joined her sisters in the élite Quaker community in Philadelphia. Although she was disowned by the reformed Quaker Meeting for marrying her cousin, Dr. Charles Moore, in 1767, subsequently moving to the country, Moore kept in touch with family and friends, circulating her manu-

Prospectus for *Liberia Herald*, Monrovia, Cape Mesurado, [West Africa], February 16, 1826. Rare Book and Special Collections Division, Library of Congress.

Along with thirty some colonists, the first emigrant ship from Boston brought generous donations for the struggling settlement at Cape Mesurado, including a printing press, blacksmith's equipment, agricultural and mechanical tools, books, medicine, and clothing. But protection from the fever could not be imported and most of the leaders of this New England group died within weeks of arrival.

Liberia Herald.

PUBLISHED AT MONROVIA, CAPE MESURADO, (WEST AFRICA.)....CHARLES L. FORCE PRINTER.

MONROVIA, (CAPE MESURADO,) THURSDAY, FEBRUARY 16, 1826.

PROSPECTUS
FOR PUBLISHING A NEWSPAPER
ENTITLED THE
LIBERIA HERALD.
To be printed at Monrovia, (Cape Mesurado.)

A printing establishment having been generously contributed by a few friends in Boston, and sent out in the brig Vine, it is deemed very important to have it go into immediate operation.

Various are the purposes which will subserve, but none appear more interesting than the regular issue of a periodical journal. A great variety of interesting intelligence is collected here from time to time, and the columns of a News-Paper furnish the best medium for the diffusion of this intelligence to all parts of the world.

To the Colony also it will be of essential service. The circulation of religious intelligence among us, the promulgation of all public notices and new laws, the decisions of courts, the arrival and departure of vessels, the notice of marriages and deaths, both in this country and America, together with a variety of political and religious essays, which may occupy its columns will furnish the means of instruction and improvement to every family and school on many important branches of knowledge.

The Editorial department is under the particular supervision of the Agent of the Colony,—But all communications must be addressed to the Printer.

CONDITIONS:

The publication will be issued once a fortnight in folio size, on fine paper with fair and handsome type, at $1,00 per annum, in advance, or $1,50 payable in six months. No paper will be discontinued until all arrearages are paid.

☞ The first number will be issued as soon as two hundred subscribers can be obtained.
CHARLES L. FORCE.

ARRIVAL OF THE NEW ENGLAND EXPEDITION.

On the 7th inst., the brig Vine, Capt. Grozer, arrived at this port in 34 days from Boston, with Colonists for Liberia. We are happy to assure our American friends that the officers and crew, the Rev. Mr. Sessions, and Rev. Mr. Holton the missionary, and Mr. Force, Printer, together with all the Colonists are in perfect health, and have been unusually protected of Heaven from the dangers of the deep, and from the attacks of disease.

They were welcomed by our citizens by the discharge of artillery, by acclamations of joy, and by crowds at the wharf, ready to conduct them to their dwellings. The landing of the people and the unloading the brig was effected without an accident. The Colonists have all been admitted as free citizens of Liberia, drawn their town lots and plantations, and been located temporarily in convenient houses generously offered them by our citizens till they can erect their own.

We understand that they are highly pleased with the healthiness and progress of the Colony, and, to use their own words, "feel that they have now got home." The Agency testified the feelings with which they received this expedition by inviting the Captain, Mr. Parker, Messrs Sessions, Holton, and Mr. Force, and all the Colonists who had come ashore, to a public dinner. Many of the citizens also formed part of the company, and the whole was conducted with great order and cheerfulness, and left a happy impression on all our minds.

We intended to have given a detailed account of the various articles so liberally contributed to the use of the Colony by our friends in New England, but we have room only for a few. The ten hhds. of first rate Kentucky leaf tobacco, purchased by the Society is a most seasonable supply, and brought without freight, and thus saved to the Society $150. The Printing press, sent out gratis also, is of the greatest value; whether we regard the enthusiastic joy with which it was received, the spirit of improvement it is likely to awake in the Colony, or the influence it will have in commending our cause to public patronage. When we call to mind these things, and learn that it was procured included salary of the Printer, at an expense of more than $1000, and cannot adequately express our gratitude to the munificent donors. But they will best understand our feelings when we inform them that nearly $200 have been subscribed by our citizens towards the immediate issue and support of a public Newspaper.

We judge also that there are received a thousand volumes of useful, and many of them most valuable books, and probably as many more pamphlets. We ought particularly to specify a complete set of the North American Review, presented by Mr. Sparks, the Editor. The forty Bibles and Testaments presented by the Massachusetts Bible Society, and the $20 amount of Tracts, presented by the New England Tract Society, the boxes from Andover, Medway, Dedham, Portland and Boston.

To this we add two sets of patent scales, two pair of Blacksmith's bellows, two anvils, and a complete establishment for a blacksmith's shop. One pair of globes, and a bell worth $40—all kinds of stationary, two chests of medicine, and a great variety of agricultural and mechanical tools, clothing, household furniture and provision; besides many private donations to all the Colonists that embarked.

If all this may be viewed as an index of the state of feeling in New England, it must be most gratifying to the American Colonization Society, and furnishes a pledge never before given, that Africa is to arise from her degradation, and this Colony to receive an impulse which no subsequent disaster can effectually check.

The Agent of the Colony returned on the 13th inst. to Monrovia, after an absence of three weeks, attended by several of the settlers, on a visit to Grand Colo, New Sesters, and Grand Bassa, for the inspection of the factories and new possessions of the Colony in that quarter. Among the objects accomplished by this excursion are the conclusion of a treaty of amity and trade with the King of Grand Colo, from which place, as the first fruits of the new arrangement, a full schooner load of rice and oil was sent by the Agent, even before his own return, to the Cape. The resources of that country are found to be abundant, and its accession to the new relation which it now sustains to the Colony, promises to the latter, important advantages. Gr. Colo, it will be perceived, from a map of the coast, is the country contiguous to the dominions of King Wilson (or West,) on the South east, whose transactions in the slave traffic are second in extent only to those Sinca of Gallinas. Trade-town the grand mart of slaves on this line of the coast, is thus brought within the stations at which the influence of the Colony may be now considered as partially established.

The Agent was induced by various reasons, not yet proper to be fully disclosed, to visit Trade-town. The number of slaves, at present waiting their dispatch at this place, is 300; the whole number had been collected in the short space of four weeks. King Wilson, having acquired his consequence by means of this traffic, discovers no inclination to abandon it for any other pursuit; and regards the progress of juster views on this subject, beginning to prevail among the adjoining tribes, with a mixture of concern and indignation.

His next neighbour, King Freeman, of New Sesters, from whom the Colony has obtained the grant of an extensive territory, and other valuable privileges, and where it has the oldest of its remote establishments, has given, in the present instance, several fresh proofs of the sincerity in which his former transactions with the Agent have been conducted. Owing to the present demand for grain and oil at Trade-town, for provisioning the slaves, and a few other impeding circumstances now believed to be happily redressed, the factory at this place was found in a less flourishing state than its beginnings had promised. But the ultimate advantages of the establishment to the Colony have determined the Agent to omit no practicable means of advancing its usefulness to the full measure of which it is certainly susceptible.

The new acquisition at Grand Bassa presents an object of the most interesting character. The factory is in complete operation—The friendship of the aristocracy of the country, (for their king's distinctive prerogatives are merely nominal) appears founded on the basis of enlightened and just views of the true interests of their people; and promise to be permanent. They offer to the Agent any extension of territory and of privileges, which he will engage to employ in founding and forwarding among them the institutions of civilized life. The limited means now at the Agent's command of executing such engagements, alone prevent the immediate conclusion of an arrangement, which, it is hoped at no distant time will direct the extension of civilization and Christianity to that interesting country with equal advantage to all descriptions of persons destined to participate in the blessings which must follow it. It is confidently expected that an invaluable acquisition of territory will very shortly be secured to the Colony in that quarter by simple purchase.

It is most gratifying to find, as the Agent has, in this excursion, an eager, desire expressed by all the leeward tribes, except Wilson's people, for the immediate establishment of schools among them for the instruction of their children in the English language and letters. It is the opinion of the Agent, that at least three schools in that quarter would be wholly supported by the King and head-men of the country, provided instructors could be furnished them. The part of the coast visited presents a population, it is believed, fully equal to any section of Western Africa in which the slave trade prevails to an equal extent; the lands are drier, and of more uniform fertility that in the immediate vicinity of the Cape; and could Christianity and the arts once gain an effectual introduction, it is not possible to picture a richer scene of moral and physical wealth and beauty than this delightful region offers to the imagination which surveys it.

Organiz d on the 16th inst. the second Trading Company of Liberia, on the basis of maximum prices and equitable trade, both with the different tribes and with foreign nations. Any traffic in human blood or spirituous liquors with the natives is a violation of the Constitution, and incurs heavy penalties.

MARRIED,
On the evening of the 14th inst., by the Rev. Mr. Sessions, Mr. Richard Sears, to Miss Rosenna Mason Fitch. All recently from America.

Drowned, at Cape Mesurado, the 9th inst. Mr. Coy Page, formerly of Richmond City, Virginia.

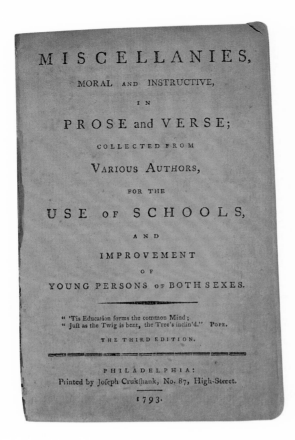

script compilations of literary commonplace books that feature women's writings on a wide range of issues beyond domestic concerns.[12] After the Revolutionary War, Moore satisfied a growing demand for printed textbooks by publishing in 1787 her *Miscellanies, Moral and Instructive*, a collection of prose and poetry selected to improve "understandings and morals" and "instructively amuse the vacant hours of young people." Mrs. Carson acquired the third edition (Philadelphia, 1793) of this popular work.

Moore's *Miscellanies* was probably required reading at the first Philadelphia charter school for girls, John Poor's Academy. *The Rise and Progress of the Young Ladies' Academy of Philadelphia* (Philadelphia, 1794), recorded in less than ten copies, describes the activities of this school, established in 1787 "to enrich the female mind while promoting Christian virtue."[13] John Poor served as principal and among the fifteen

members of the board of trustees were Rev. James Sproat, president; Benjamin Say, secretary; Pelatiah Webster, William Coates, and Benjamin West. While acknowledging that most of the scholars were from the Philadelphia area, the administration proudly announced that its alumnae included girls from every state, as well as Canada and the West Indies.[14] Complementing this account is *A Collection of Psalms and Hymns*, compiled by John Poor in 1794 for the use of the Young Ladies' Academy, where in the preface he declares, "The song of praise is an act of devotion; joy is the natural effect of praise, and song the proper accompaniment of joy."

Advice books and guides to conduct include such titles as Hannah More's *Thoughts on the Importance of Manners of the Great to General Society* (Philadelphia, 1788); John Witherspoon's *Series of Letters on Education* (New York, 1797); Thomas Gisborne's

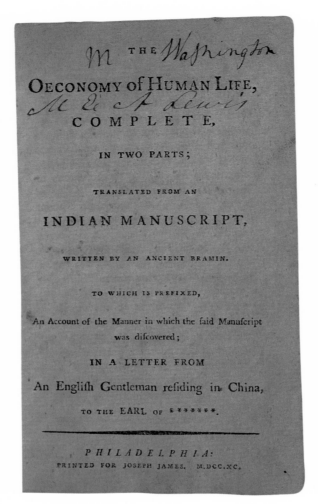

THE Washington

OECONOMY of HUMAN LIFE,
M & A Lewis
C O M P L E T E,

IN TWO PARTS;

TRANSLATED FROM AN

INDIAN MANUSCRIPT,

WRITTEN BY AN ANCIENT BRAMIN.

TO WHICH IS PREFIXED,

An Account of the Manner in which the said Manuscript was discovered;

IN A LETTER FROM

An English Gentleman residing in China,

TO THE EARL OF *******.

PHILADELPHIA:
PRINTED FOR JOSEPH JAMES. M.DCC.XC.

Enquiry into the Duties of the Female Sex (Philadelphia, 1798)—William Davis's copy; and John Gregory's *Father's Legacy to his Daughters* (Philadelphia, 1798). Of special note is Martha Washington's copy of the 1790 Philadelphia edition of *The Oeconomy of Human Life,* a popular compilation of maxims first published in London in 1750, written by Philip Stanhope, Earl of Chesterfield, but sometimes attributed to Robert Dodsley.[15]

Amongst several rare almanacs in the Carson Collection is the first volume of *The American Ladies Pocket Book* (Philadelphia, 1796). In his address to readers, publisher W. Y. Birch announces that this

new work for the ladies of America is intended for usefulness as well as amusement and encourages women to submit original poetry and word puzzles for inclusion in subsequent annuals. This copy, once owned by John McAllister, Jr., features a James Thackara frontispiece depicting "Memory" recording the amusements of time and is known in only four copies. The volume for the year 1820 features engravings of Philadelphia, New York, and Boston scenes by Thomas Birch, Thomas Doughty, and others and includes selected prose, poetry, songs, dances, word puzzles, and monetary tables.

It is a challenge to bring something new to the Library's unmatched gastronomy collections, but among the nearly thirty books on cookery and culinary arts assembled by Marian Carson are several such items. In *The Art of Dining; and, the Art of Attaining High Health* (Philadelphia, 1837), Thomas Walker stresses the importance of eating in moderation and of regular exercise and offers etiquette advice to smokers. The rare *Complete Confectioner, Pastry-Cook, and Baker* (Philadelphia, 1844) eluded cookbook collector Katherine Bitting and is reported in less than ten copies. In her preface, Eleanor Parkinson explains that although the confectionery art is the "poetry of epicurism," it is still much neglected in the United States. By making alterations and additions to a popular London publication, she presents five hundred recipes for sugar-boiling, comfits, lozenges, ornamental cakes, meringues, compotes, and tarts. An advertisement for Parkinson's Chestnut Street confectionery shop proposes to supply public and private balls, picnics, and wedding entertainments. Several Carson cookbooks were previously owned by men, notably John McAllister's copies of Hannah Glasse's *Art of Cookery* (Dublin, 1799) and Eliza Leslie's *Seventy-five Receipts* (Boston, 1836); and Julius Sachse's copy of *Die Geschickte Hausfrau* (Harrisburg, Pennsylvania, 1851).

Another rarity, recorded in only three copies, is *Camp Cookery and Hospital Diet* (New York, 1861). Asserting that "A wretched diet will demoralize an army, and destroy it quicker than the bullets of an enemy," this cooking manual borrows from recipes

Camp Cookery and Hospital Diet for the Use of the U.S. Volunteers now in Service **(New York, 1861), title page.** *U.S. Army General Hospital, Thanksgiving Dinner, Thursday, November 24, 1864,* **menu. Rare Book and Special Collections Division, Library of Congress. Photograph by Edward Owen.**

By telling us something about food preparation during the Civil War, this military cooking manual and hospital menu offer a window on at least one aspect of the everyday life of a soldier.

developed by British culinary expert Alexis Soyer during the Crimean War that suggest simple healthy fare for fifty or more men on the march, as well as special dishes designed for those convalescing in military hospitals. Another rare bit of ephemera, the 1864 Thanksgiving dinner menu for a Union Army hospital, shows real effort to honor this national observance established by Lincoln the previous year, despite the sufferings of war.

Marian Carson's life-long passion for the decorative arts is reflected by a number of works on architecture. Particularly notable is a collection of architectural plates, *Designs in Architecture* by John Soane (London, 1778), "for temples, baths, cassines, pavilions, garden-seats, obelisks, and other buildings, for decorating pleasure-ground, parks, forests, &c."[16] Another work new to the Library is the rare 1838 *Panorama and Views of Philadelphia*, in light original color, and bound in ribbon-embossed cloth. John Caspar Wild, a leader in early lithography in Philadelphia, produced four panorama views from the State House steeple, giving an excellent overview of the physical layout of Philadelphia in the 1830s (see page 2).[17]

Interests in the decorative arts and education intersect in Mrs. Carson's strong showing of drawing and penmanship books. Among nearly four dozen works on drawing are introductory manuals and juvenile copybooks, as well as fine hand-colored specimen books for craftsmen. Popular works by drawing masters Rembrandt Peale and John Rubens Smith complement the earlier basic work of James Thackara. Many of these titles are new to the Library's holdings, including three early-nineteenth-century works featuring techniques of flower painting in watercolors, with splendid illustrations. Among the baker's dozen penmanship books are at least three of special interest. The oldest and most elaborate is Johann Schirmer's *Geöfnete Schreib-Schule* (Frankfurt, 1760), reported in only three copies. In addition to analyzing penmanship, it illustrates the art of flourishing, using intricate calligraphy to reproduce animals and landscapes. John Jenkins' *Art of Writing*, printed in Boston in 1791 by Isaiah Thomas and Ebenezer Andrews, is reported in only eight copies. Carson's copy of *Becker's Ornamental Penmanship; a Series of Analytical and Finished Alphabets* (Philadelphia, 1855) is bound in a preliminary state of eleven sheets, with three uncut leaves per sheet. Manuscript testimonials and reviews on the 1877 edition are pasted in. George Becker, professor of drawing, writing, and bookkeeping at Girard College, stresses the need for mathematical precision in forming lettering and notes its importance to such vocations as bookkeeping, engraving, stone-cutting, and bookbinding.

Marian Carson's special fascination with collecting children's literature, combined with her interest in the decorative arts and early American printing, has brought to the Library a splendid gathering of rare and fragile little pieces, printed primarily in Philadelphia and New York during the first half of the nineteenth century. Through charming verse and delightful illustration these tiny survivors document the emerging emphasis on reading for pleasure and entertainment rather than exclusively for moral instruction and help us to better understand the minds of the adults that produced them.

John Rubens Smith, **Perspectival drawings of buildings**, lithograph from Smith, *The Juvenile Drawing-Book* (Philadelphia, 1854). Rare Book and Special Collections Division, Library of Congress. *First published in 1839, this popular work by the accomplished drawing master presented the basic elements of perspective, drawing, and shading.*

John Soane, "Seat for a Flower Garden," plate III from Soane, *Designs in Architecture* (London, 1778). Rare Book and Special Collections Division, Library of Congress. *Soane considered this portfolio of drawings, published while he was a student, to be of little merit and later he attempted to buy and destroy all known copies. After studying in Italy and directing major public renovation projects in London, he became professor of architecture at the Royal Academy.*

Johann Michael Schirmer, *Geöfnete Schreib-Schule* ([Frankfurt, 1760?]), title page. Rare Book and Special Collections Division, Library of Congress. *This scarce work on German calligraphy is the earliest of thirteen penmanship books collected by Mrs. Carson.*

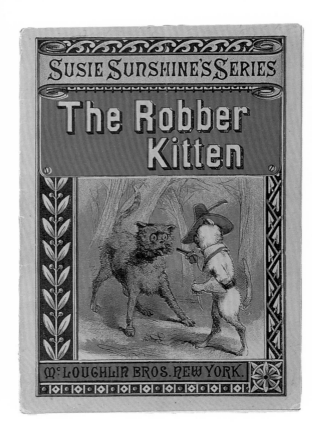

The Robber Kitten (New York, 186-?); *A Missionary Present about the Red Children* (London, ca. 1872); *Kate Greenaway's Alphabet* (New York, [1885])—given to Joseph Carson by his grandmother in 1886; *Boys' Own Picture Book, with Pictures* (Cincinnati, 183-?); *Juvenile Pastimes, or, Girls' and Boys' Book of Sports* (New Haven, 1849).

OPPOSITE
In the Forest (Boston, 1865); *Youthful Sports* (New York, [1825-1833]); *The Young Child's ABC, or First Book* (New York, 1806); *The Farm* (Philadelphia, ca. 1813); [Avis C. *Howland*], *Rhode-Island Tales* (New York, 1830). Rare Book and Special Collections Division, Library of Congress. Photograph by Edward Owen.

This sampling of tiny survivors created to instruct and amuse yesterday's children, shows a range of subjects and cover illustrations spanning eighty years of the nineteenth century.

The Royal Primer, reprinted by John Dunlap (Philadelphia, 1770), offers sound advice to young readers: "He who ne'er learns his A, B, C, Forever will a Blockhead be; But he who to his Books inclin'd, will soon a golden Treasure find." *The Young Child's A B C, or First Book* (New York, 1806) is the first of many thousands of children's books printed by Samuel Wood. It is doubly precious because the illustrations are by Alexander Anderson, the father of woodcutting in America. Carson brings seven new Samuel Wood items to the Library, as well as more than one hundred and fifty other juvenile titles not previously in our collections. The chapbook *Youthful Sports* (New York, [1825-1833]), celebrating the health benefits of outdoor recreation, is one of many such pieces, illustrated with simple and amusing woodcuts and both printed and sold by Mahlon Day. Carson brings nine new Mahlon Day works to the Library. *Marmaduke Multiply* (Boston, 1839), one of several

illustrated primers, is bound in an extremely rare ribbon-embossed cloth cover. The delightful border illustrations in *Juvenile Pastimes* (New Haven, Connecticut, 1849) feature a variety of activities being enjoyed separately, as well as by both sexes. The fragile *In the Forest* (Boston, 1865), folded in accordion fashion, depicts the sights and sounds of the forest on a summer night through chromolithographic illustrations typical of works by the Boston publisher L. Prang, and is one of five Prangs collected by Marian Carson. The only known surviving copy of *A Missionary Present about the Red Children* (London, ca. 1872) is an illustrated description of Native American children's lives and customs written for children of European descent and distributed by the Wesleyan Methodist Missionary Society.[18]

Another unique piece, probably published in London, is a stylized, three-dimensional view of what appears to be Trafalgar Square. Six plates are

connected by folded, accordion-style sheets with three
peep holes through which the scene may be viewed
from different angles. We know that Mrs. Carson
acquired this intriguing item with the McAllister collection, for Janet McAllister tried to mend the fragile
accordion sheets with her address stickers.[19]

Among over thirty games and amusements for
children collected by Mrs. Carson are puzzles, blocks,
and numerous board, card, and word games related
to such diverse subjects as literary authors, travel,
and war. Two of the twelve foreign games are
metamorphoses, permitting players to create various
transformations by substituting moveable parts.
Changeable Ladies (London, 1819) includes twenty-
eight sets of cards with human profiles of inter-
changeable foreheads, noses, and chins featuring a
variety of costumes and hairdressing that "will produce an old friend with a new face" or "provide
samples for matrimonial choice."

The few European items in Carson's children's
collection tend to be striking and unusual, as is true

of *L'Empire de la Reine des Fleurs* or *The Realm of the
Queen of Flowers* ([France?, 188-?]), which promises
"rational entertainment" in forming an endless variety
of bouquets from this portfolio of fifty hand-
colored, lithographed paper flowers and four slitted
cards illustrated with vases. The instruction booklet,
printed in French, German, and English, gives the
name and meaning of each flower and suggests
that the more elegant compositions could be used
as models for drawing, painting, or embroidery.

With her passion and perseverance, Marian
Carson gathered an impressive body of printed material that celebrates the social diversity of American
life while documenting the political, cultural, and
economic growth of the American Republic during
its first century. In making the Carson Collection of
printed materials accessible to the nation, the Rare
Book and Special Collections Division joins Marian
Carson in encouraging its use in developing new
insights into our American past.

Changeable Ladies
(London, 1819). Rare Book
and Special Collections
Division, Library of
Congress. Photograph
by Edward Owen.
*Providing a glimpse of
hair and clothing styles of
another era, this game of
transformation is one of over
thirty children's games and
amusements assembled by
Marian Carson.*

L'empire de la Reine des Fleurs.

Récréation raisonnée

offerte par l'assemblage mille fois varié des plus jolies fleurs, pour en former des bouquets, des couronnes etc.

V. Édition.

Les diverses fleurs choisies et pratiquées dans l'un des 4 cartons ci-joints, en ce qu'on en introduit la queue dans les fentes que portent ces cartons — formeront aussitôt les plus gracieux bouquets et les plus élégants, et cela au gré et selon le goût de l'amateur, selon les saisons qui font éclore ces fleurs et enfin, selon l'intention significative qu'on apportera à ce charmant ouvrage. Dans ce dernier cas, le devise, que le texte ajoute au nom de chaque fleur, pourra servir de guide. C'est ainsi, par exemple que les lettres initiales des fleurs mêmes, pourront former un nom ou un mot quelconque qu'il sera fort intéressant d'étudier et de deviner. Les Numéros exposés sur la queue de chaque fleur, correspondant au Numéro et au sens de chacune d'elles. Une semblable composition élégante et fait avec goût, soit pour les formes, les couleurs et la signification, pourra servir de modèle au dessinateur, au peintre et même pour la broderie.

Nous conseillons au compositeur d'un semblable tableau de commencer par la partie haute du carton, à introduire la queue des fleurs, de

Das Reich der Blumenkönigin.

Sinnige Unterhaltung

durch Zusammenstellung der schönsten Zierpflanzen zu Bouquets und Kränzen in tausendfacher Veränderung.

V. Auflage.

Die einzelnen Blumen werden, auf einem der 4 Cartons in die darin angebrachten Einschnitte gesteckt, und dadurch die anmuthigsten Kränze und Bouquets geformt, entweder nach freier Wahl der Blumen, oder je nach der Jahreszeit, in welcher sie blühen, oder nach dem Sinn ihrer Bedeutung. Zu letzterem Zweck dient auch im Text dem Namen jeder Blume beigefügte Motto. — Nach den Anfangsbuchstaben der Blumen lassen sich Namen, Worte etc. zusammenstellen, deren Errathung zur angenehmen Unterhaltung dient. — Die Nummern und die Bedeutung derselben auf den Stiel der Blumen verweisen auf die Nummer im Text unter gleicher Nummer. — Ein in der Zusammenstellung geschmackvolles Tableau wird als Verlage zum Nachzeichnen und Malen dienen, sowie Stern zu Masten für Plattstickereien geben.

Bei Zusammenstellung eines Tableau ist es rathsam, mit dem Einstecken der Blumen am oberen Ende des Cartons zu beginnen, und damit

The Realm of the QUEEN OF FLOWERS.

Rational entertainment

by forming bouquets and garlands in endless variation from the most beautiful flowers.

V. Edition.

The several flowers are placed on one of the 4 Cartons in the incision made for this purpose; thus the most elegant bouquets and garlands are produced either according to free choice of the flowers, or the time of the year in which they bloom, or their symbolic signification as given here. For the latter purpose is used the motto attached to the name of each flower in the text. From the first letters of the flowers, words and names can be composed, the unriddling of which affords most agreeable amusement. The numbers on the stalks of the flowers refer to the name and signification of the same in the text and to the same number. — Such a composition made with taste and elegance will serve as a model for drawing and painting, and even for embroidery.

In the composition of a tableau it is advisable to begin with inserting the flowers in the upper end of the carton, to continue farther

44

36

18.

14.

37.

34.

1. Gerd-J. Bötte and Werner Tannhof, *The First Century of German Language Printing in the United States of America* (Göttingen, 1989), #196.

2. Julius F. Sachse, "Kelpius's 'Method of Prayer,'" *Pennsylvania-German Society. Proceedings and Addresses*, 25 (1917), 95-100.

3. Julius F. Sachse, *German Sectarians of Pennsylvania* (Philadelphia, 1899, reprinted 1971), 2 vols., 1:146. Bötte and Tannhof, *German Language Printing*, #1.

4. Sachse, *German Sectarians of Pennsylvania*, 1: 184-87. See also Library Company of Philadelphia, *Germantown and the Germans* (Philadelphia, 1983), 74.

5. Bötte and Tannhof, *German Language Printing*, #10.

6. The erudite James Logan had prepared this translation with instructive and entertaining notes about ten years earlier when he was sixty, having retired to his books from his former public responsibilities as secretary to William Penn and mayor of Philadelphia.

7. Marian Carson gave some information about this treasure-bearing side trip from the Catskills in "Medical Bottles, Vials, and Other Equipment," *New York History*, January 1954, but did not mention finding the broadside. In her interview with Library curators, September 16, 1996, she described finding the broadside in the same Dutch farmhouse, along with a list of medicines of the 1790s. In order of printing, Michael J. Walsh places the Carson broadside as number six. Loudon printed the Declaration in his *New York Packet* on July 11, 1776. See Walsh, "Contemporary Broadside Editions of the Declaration of Independence," *Harvard Library Bulletin*, 3 (1949), 31-43.

8. The publication of this address was countered by the publication of extracts from "testimonies" and "epistles" presented at various Quaker meetings held in 1775-77.

9. Of particular associational interest are William McAllister catalogs for eyeglasses, microscopes, and optical instruments; George Pierce catalogs for magic lantern projections; and James Queen catalogs for optical and astronomical instruments.

10. For an extensive study of this yellow fever crisis, see J. H. Powell, *Bring Out Your Dead* (Philadelphia, 1993), 95-101. It was originally published ca. 1949, with acknowledgment for the help of Mr. and Mrs. Joseph Carson.

11. The newspaper by the same name, established by John B. Russwurm in 1830, was a strict American Colonization Society organ much different than the free press journal envisioned by the Force prospectus. See P. J. Staudenraus, *The African Colonization Movement*, 1816-1865 (New York, 1961, reprinted 1980), 123-24, 191.

12. For a comprehensive study of Moore's literary manuscript compilations, as well as an analysis of her printed work, see Catherine Blecki and Karin A. Wulf, eds., *Milcah Martha Moore's Book* (University Park, Pennsylvania, 1997), xiv-xv, 69-75.

13. Statements regarding the number of extant copies here and below are based on a search of OCLC and RLIN online databases and *National Union Catalog, Pre-1956 Imprints*. Numbers are offered as an indication of scarcity and are not intended to be definitive.

14. This account also includes valedictory addresses, student poetry, and lists of honor students by name, (i.e. Mary Ann McPherson, English Grammar, June 1788) as well as the charter and by-laws of the corporation. An interesting tie-in with the Wetherill Papers collected by Mrs. Carson, and now in the Manuscript Division, lies in the fact that John Poor's Academy spent its first year (1788-89) on the second floor of the Free Quaker Meeting House. Dr. Benjamin Say loaned the Meeting £10 toward the cost of constructing the new floor.

15. In addition to Martha Washington's signature on the title page, other manuscript inscriptions document that this volume was later owned by George H. Nye of Lewiston, Maine, Bvt. Major General, U.S. Volunteers, during the Civil War.

16. Carson's copy has two portraits of the author laid in and bears the bookplate and inscription of William Hamilton, an amateur architect who influenced Philadelphia furniture design.

17. Complementing the panoramas are a collection of twenty views featuring individual buildings, including the Fairmount Water Works, Girard College, Pennsylvania Hospital, Christ Church, and Market Street. Each view is accompanied by a detailed historical and architectural note and a special poem.

18. An engraved portrait of Rev. Samson Occum, Indian preacher, dated 1808, is laid in the Carson copy.

19. John McAllister, Jr. (1786-1877) retired from the family optical business in 1835 and devoted the remainder of his long life to his antiquarian interests, including compiling an important library, principally relating to Philadelphia history. See Joseph Jackson, *Encyclopedia of Philadelphia* (Harrisburg, Pennsylvania, 1932) III, 882-3.

Prints and Drawings

by Harry L. Katz

Curator, Popular & Applied Graphic Art, Prints and Photographs Division, Library of Congress

OPPOSITE

(detail) John Rubens Smith, *Mill on the Brandywine.* Watercolor on paper, ca. 1828. See page 80.

Marian Carson, through her family's and her own perspicacious collecting, assembled an extraordinary array of visual materials documenting the nation's first century. From the Colonial period through the Centennial her collection documents notable figures, places, events and episodes, topics and themes in American history. To her collecting Mrs. Carson brought a discerning eye and keen awareness of the intersection where art and history meet; she acquired and preserved prints and drawings as much for the historical evidence they reveal as for their aesthetic qualities. Testaments to her knowledge and ability are found in the numerous instances in which both art and history are well served by the images she gathered.

Prints and drawings in the Carson Collection include individual items and whole archives of great significance to the study of American art history. Although Charles de Saint-Mémin's unique memorial portrait drawing of George Washington has been exhibited and published, other important works in the collection are largely unexamined and unknown. The bodies of works by John Rubens Smith, Thomas Birch, and James Queen span the nineteenth century and contain materials critical to the study of their careers and contributions to American art. The reputation of John Rubens Smith, in particular, stands in need of a reassessment as his often disagreeable

nature and persistent feuding with fellow artists and publishers led to financial hardship and historical obscurity.

Other compelling works or groups of works include a rare impression of Amos Doolittle's engraving *A Display of the United States of America*, an apparent self-portrait by Gilbert Stuart, two drawings of historical subjects by Mather Brown, a design for a coin with a head of Columbia by Henry Inman, and an unpublished set of eighteen Civil War watercolors by William McIlvaine, Jr. Marian Carson collected and preserved Civil War imagery in depth, as well as images related to such topics as African American history, women, advertising, the Fairmount Waterworks near Philadelphia, and the United States Centennial Exposition. Together with the larger bodies of works by Birch, Smith, and Queen, these holdings form a composite portrait of the young American republic and its efforts to create a unified nation.

The image of George Washington was central to the republic's new identity. He led the American army to victory over the British, served as head of the Constitutional Convention, won election as the first president of the United States, and served two terms. He became a symbol of America during his lifetime and portrayals of his likeness wearing military, civilian, or antique garb were ubiquitous. Two particularly

Amos Doolittle, *A Display of the United States of America*. Engraving on paper (sixth or seventh state), 1794. Prints and Photographs Division, Library of Congress (LC-USZC4-6720).

Begun in late 1788 or early 1789 and considered one of the earliest American presidential political prints, this rare engraved portrait of George Washington went through numerous editions as its creator, New Haven printmaker Amos Doolittle (1754–1832), adjusted publication dates and state population figures to keep the image current through the first president's two terms in office.

important Washington portraits, one rare and the other unique, are preserved in the Carson Collection.

The rare work is Amos Doolittle's engraving entitled *A Display of the United States of America*, featuring a central profile portrait of Washington surrounded by a linked ring of state seals. The text proudly commemorates the Declaration of Independence and the Constitution, and identifies Washington as "The Protector of his COUNTRY, and the Supporter of the rights of MANKIND." Doolittle, an enterprising printer and engraver in New Haven, Connecticut, exploited the commercial potential of Washington's likeness following the 1788 election, the country's first presidential campaign, to create one of the earliest American presidential political prints.[1] This unusually large and ambitious print by a native-born, apparently self-taught engraver represented a significant achievement in American popular printmaking and marked George Washington's passage from military command to civilian rule.[2] The engraving proved commercially successful and Doolittle later created similar engravings portraying John Adams and Thomas Jefferson.

Charles Balthazar Julien Fevret de Saint-Mémin (1770–1852), who fled the French Revolution with his aristocratic family and settled in New York City, was one of the most meticulous, elegant, and prolific portraitists in America in 1799, the year George Washington died. To eulogize the late president, Saint-Mémin created a unique memorial portrait which reflected modern theories, tools, and techniques but evoked Antiquity (see page 4). His choice of the profile format was inspired both by contemporary writings of Johann Kaspar Lavater and the art of ancient Greece. Lavater's theories on physiognomy held that a people's moral character and intellectual capabilities are revealed in the contours of their skull and facial features. His views were widely accepted during the late eighteenth century, and profile portraits were thought to be the best means of displaying cranial structure. Furthermore, recent excavations of

Greek antiquities showed that profile portraits were a favored means of portraying leaders of that early democratic society, which served as a self-conscious model for the new American republic. The laurel wreath signifying Washington's military victories and Saint-Mémin's deliberate imitation in two dimensions of a three-dimensional sculptured classical bas-relief are further allusions to Antiquity. Saint-Mémin is believed to have drawn this portrait from a life mask of Washington, employing a mechanical device called a physiognotrace, used by artists of the period to create extremely accurate depictions of their subjects. He combined these varied theories, techniques, and instruments to produce a memorial portrait of uncommon accuracy, strength, and monumentality.[3]

The Saint-Mémin drawing first came into the possession of the Carson family during the nineteenth century when, over more than thirty years, Hampton L. Carson assembled one of the largest private collections of prints and drawings in America. His portrait holdings encompassed United States presidents, signers of the Declaration of Independence, members of Congress, military officers, and foreign dignitaries. In 1898, he acquired a spectacular collection of 761 medallion portrait engravings by Saint-Mémin formerly in the possession of New York picture dealer Elias Dexter. Saint-Mémin routinely retained proof impressions of his engravings to show prospective clients and built several large sets of his own graphic work, which were sold intact to individuals after his death. The set acquired by Hampton Carson in 1898 is now preserved at the National Gallery in Washington, D.C., where it is recognized as the second largest set of Saint-Mémin engravings in existence (the largest, comprised of 818 portrait engravings and related works, is also in Washington, at the Corcoran Gallery of Art).[4] In 1903, Hampton Carson decided to disperse his entire print collection at auction. In a letter to the auctioneer printed in the sale catalogue he

Gilbert Stuart (attributed), [Self-Portrait]. Ink and wash on paper, ca. 1783. Prints and Photographs Division, Library of Congress (LC-USZC4-6721).

In 1783, when this sketch is thought to have been made, Gilbert Stuart was in London exhibiting numerous works at the British Royal Academy and embarking on his subsequent illustrious career as America's foremost portraitist.

described the burden of labor imposed by authors and publishers requesting the use of images from his collection:

These requests are being renewed constantly in different directions and it has become an impossibility, with the pressure of professional and public duty, to adequately care for it and reply to the numerous demands, for essentially it makes me a curator of a public institution without the leisure to attend to it.

Will you not therefore at your convenience have the pictures catalogued, properly advertised and sold?

It would be fortunate if some institution could acquire them, as they must grow in value and in national interest with every year, illustrating the history of our country as nothing else can do, and it is now impossible to reconstruct another collection containing precisely the same subjects.[5]

The sale of the Hampton L. Carson Collection began in January 1904 with his Washington portraits, including the Saint-Mémin set and memorial portrait.[6] Unfortunately, no public institution came forward to purchase the entire collection and the portraits were sold at prices ranging from twenty-five cents for individual engravings to forty-eight hundred dollars for the set of Saint-Mémins that now resides at the National Gallery of Art. The memorial profile drawing went to the same bidder, the publisher William J. Campbell, for eight hundred dollars. Ultimately, the Saint-Mémin crayon drawing returned to the Carson family some time after 1926, when Joseph Carson acquired it from an unidentified Pennsylvania collector.[7]

The Carson Collection also includes other eighteenth-century drawings by important American artists. Celebrated portrait painter Gilbert Stuart is represented in the Carson Collection by a small, delicate ink sketch said to be a self-portrait. Stuart (1755-1828) sailed for London and the tutelage of fellow American Benjamin West, then President of the English Royal Academy, in summer 1775. By 1783, when this sketch is thought to have been made, he had exhibited numerous works at the Royal Academy exhibitions and become a member of the

Baptism of Edward 1st

Incorporated Society of Artists. He went on to
become the most celebrated portrait painter in
America. The drawing is unsigned, but the aged
mount to which it is affixed bears the inscription,
"Portrait of Gilbert Stuart drawn in 1783 by himself
and given to Thomas Sully about 1817[,] from Sully to
J R Lambdin 1857." Thomas Sully (1783-1872) inherited Stuart's mantle as the country's leading portraitist,
while James Reid Lambdin (1807-1889) studied under
Sully and became a noted painter of portraits and
miniatures in Philadelphia.

Two drawings of historical subjects by Stuart's
contemporary, the expatriate American artist Mather
Brown (1761-1831), were acquired about 1942 by
Marian and Joseph Carson. Born in Boston, Brown
studied there with Stuart and in 1781 he too traveled
to London to study at the Royal Academy under
West. Within two years he also had exhibited paintings at the Academy and embarked on a promising
career. Unlike Stuart, who returned to America,
Brown remained in England to his death. During
West's tenure in the last decades of the eighteenth

century, grand historical subjects derived from the Bible, mythology, great battles, or scenes from Shakespearean tragedies, were among the few themes considered suitable for academic artists. Brown's work from this period is represented in the Carson Collection by drawings portraying scenes from the life of Julius Caesar and King Edward I.[8]

Henry Inman (1801-1846) carried on the tradition of American portraiture well into the mid-nineteenth century. Trained in the art as apprentice to John Wesley Jarvis in New York City, he established an independent career there and by 1830 had achieved such stature that he was named acting president of the National Academy of Design upon the departure of Samuel F. B. Morse for Europe. Over the course of his career Inman produced numerous large-scale portraits as well as delicate miniatures of wealthy patrons and their families. To supplement his income he drew designs for lithographed certificates and engraved banknotes. In 1933, Joseph Carson acquired from his mother's estate an oil sketch by Inman of a design for a United States coin featuring a profile head of

Columbia, symbol of the republic (see page 12).[9] This delightful small oil sketch by an accomplished American artist delineates the thin line drawn in the nineteenth century between fine and applied art. It also supports the Carson family's assemblage of visual and textual materials related to American commerce and industry.

Nineteenth-century American documentary drawings represent a great strength of the Carson Collection, the result of Marian Carson's particular interest in the field.[10] The holdings range from single drawings to whole artists' archives, gathered by Mrs. Carson both to document their achievements and activities and to preserve a vital record of how America looked in the decades before photography became commonplace. The archives of works by Thomas Birch, James Queen, and John Rubens Smith offer hundreds of unpublished, rarely seen views of American cities, towns, and rural areas. They vividly portray their times and illuminate the history of American graphic art, its technical development, and aesthetic progress. In addition to these archives, works by F. O. C. Darley, Augustus Kollner, J. J. Barralet, G. R. Bonfield, C. R. Leslie, John A. Woodside, and others are in the collection.

Thomas Birch (1779-1851), son of the noted artist and Philadelphia delineator William Russell Birch, established a fine reputation in his own right as a painter of marine subjects, in particular his portrayals of notable naval battles of the War of 1812. Birch met the market for images of the conflict with numerous paintings, prints, and drawings. In 1996, Marian Carson gave to the Library Birch's ink and wash drawing of the Battle of Lake Erie (see page 16). Fought September 10, 1813, the confrontation pitted American ships led by master commandant Oliver Hazard Perry against a desperate British fleet. Perry's crushing victory proved a turning point in the war, inspired Americans, and spurred a lively trade in images of the contest. The Carson Collection drawing reproduces with minor changes one of Birch's most celebrated paintings, a depiction of the engagement between *USS Niagara* and *HMS Queen Charlotte*, now in the collection of the Pennsylvania

Academy of the Fine Arts.[11] The drawing probably served as a model for engraver Alexander Lawson, who apparently published a print after the painting.[12]

Along with the Lake Erie drawing, the Carson Collection contains a portfolio comprised of approximately forty drawings and seventeen prints by Birch, along with photographs of paintings and manuscripts related to his career.[13] Created by Mrs. Carson in pursuit of her personal interest in the Birch family of painters, the portfolio contains pencil and watercolor drawings, including sketches from nature and initial studies for more finished works.

If the Thomas Birch drawings provide an intimate glimpse into his world, the John Rubens Smith drawings provide a panoramic view.[14] They include more than two hundred pencil and watercolor sketches of American cities and towns, street scenes, bridges, buildings and monuments, mills and factories, churches, rivers, and streams Smith rendered in his travels. Between 1809 and 1844, Smith journeyed the length of the Eastern seaboard, sketching American cities, towns, and landscapes, pursuing an unfulfilled

LEFT

Thomas Birch, [Five sketches]. Pencil, ink, and watercolor on paper mounted on brown paper, n.d. Prints and Photographs Division, Library of Congress (LC-USZC4-6674).

These selections from a large portfolio of diverse drawings, studies, and sketches by Birch offer an intimate glimpse at his personal art and working methods.

RIGHT

Thomas Birch, *Constitution and Java*, 2nd view. Ink and wash on paper, ca. 1813. Prints and Photographs Division, Library of Congress (LC-USZC4-6671).

The War of 1812 battle between USS Constitution *and the British frigate* Java *took place on December 29, 1812, off the coast of Brazil. After three hours of intense naval warfare, during which American Commodore William Bainbridge was twice wounded and the English captain mortally struck, the* Constitution *pounded the virtually dismasted* Java *into submission and surrender.*

John Rubens Smith, *Mill on the Brandywine.* Watercolor on paper, ca. 1828. Prints and Photographs Division, Library of Congress (LC-USZC4-3670). This photograph by Asman Custom Photo.

Between 1809 and 1844, painter and printmaker John Rubens Smith travelled the eastern seaboard of the United States, creating a life portrait of the young republic. His views offer a visual metaphor for the harmony between nature and industry that the new nation had achieved.

John Rubens Smith, Self-portrait. Watercolor on paper, ca. 1809. Prints and Photographs Division, Library of Congress (LC-USZC4-5640). This photograph by Asman Custom Photo.

John Rubens Smith was a skillful delineator of the American scene in the decades before photography, and a gifted teacher who influenced a generation of American artists through his drawing academies and widely published drawing manuals.

ambition to publish a portfolio of engraved American views. Most of the drawings were never published and remain largely unknown to researchers. Working during the decades before photography, Smith recorded the American scene with great skill, elegance, and accuracy. He captured the spirit and energy of the nation at a time of enormous growth and optimism, and his drawings document the transformation of the American landscape under the impact of the Industrial Revolution.

John Rubens Smith (1775-1849) was a critical, if controversial, figure in the American art community during the first half of the nineteenth century. He was the son of John Raphael Smith, England's leading printmaker, and grandson of noted landscape painter Thomas Smith of Derby. He trained in his father's studio and later studied at the Royal Academy in London where, between 1796 and 1811, he exhibited forty-five works. In 1806, at the age of thirty-one, he immigrated to the United States, convinced by an

earlier visit that opportunities were there for a man of his extraordinary sophistication and varied talents.[15]

In America, armed with letters of introduction from Benjamin West and Washington Allston, he settled in Boston, married, and soon opened a drawing academy. Through the ensuing decades he established similar academies in New York, Philadelphia, and, intermittently, at Charleston, South Carolina. Among his more notable pupils were Sanford Robinson Gifford, William Guy Wall, and Emmanuel Leutze, while Thomas Sully and Thomas Cummings also benefitted from his instruction and praised his teaching methods. Through personal instruction at his academies and such enormously influential drawing manuals and treatises as *Key to the Art of Drawing the Human Figure* (1831) and *The Juvenile Drawing-Book* (1843) (see pages 64-65), Smith became one of the country's foremost drawing masters and a principal instructor of the generation of American artists that gave rise to the Hudson River School.

Smith was renowned for his ability to teach the principles of perspective and numerous drawings in the collection attest to his skill in applying those principles to his own work. Of particular value to researchers in this regard are the series of views he made in Washington, D.C., during an extended tour of the mid-Atlantic states in 1828. He produced finished and unfinished, pencil and watercolor views of the U.S. Capitol, recording details of the building and grounds at a time when its construction under the direction of architect Charles Bulfinch was near completion (see page 24). His pencil studies of the White House are rendered so accurately they appear as measured drawings. In Albany, Boston, Providence, New York, Philadelphia, Washington, D.C., Charleston, and points in between, Smith created city views which are among the finest surviving images we have of urban America in the first half of the nineteenth century.

In addition to city views, Smith recorded the richness of American rural scenery. His renderings of the American countryside encompass the natural features of the Hudson and Passaic Rivers in New York and New Jersey, the myth-laden regions of Washington Irving's upstate New York, and suburban estates along the Brandywine and Potomac Rivers. Instructed by his father and the British Royal Academy in the picturesque tradition of English topographical draftsmanship, Smith's careful study of perspective and delicate, luminous watercolor palette lend his works a correctness and refinement matched by few of his contemporaries in the United States.

Unfortunately, however gifted Smith was as teacher and artist, he was a terrible businessman, unable to manage money and contentious to a fault. Unlike such contemporaries as John James Audubon, William Bennett, and William Birch, Smith never accomplished his ambition to produce a portfolio of engraved American views.[16] He helped conceive the landmark *Hudson River Portfolio* but was dismissed shortly after its inception and never had another opportunity to work on such a project.[17] In 1816, he alienated the entire membership of the American Academy of Art in New York, and precipitated his own firing as its curator of collections, by demanding on behalf of his young pupils and their parents the removal of his friend John Vanderlyn's

John Rubens Smith, *Cadets' Monument at West Point.*
Etching with watercolor on paper, ca. 1820. Prints and
Photographs Division, Library of Congress (LC-USZC4-3669).
The Cadet Monument in the West Point Cemetery overlooking the
Hudson River was erected by cadets and officers in memory of a
cadet who was killed by the premature discharge of a cannon in 1817.
Fifteen years earlier, the United States Military Academy was
established on the site of the garrison of American revolutionary troops
made famous by the treachery of Benedict Arnold.

John Rubens Smith after John Rowson Smith, Jr., *View of Pottsville.* **Etching with aquatint and watercolor, 1833. Prints and Photographs Division, Library of Congress (LC-USZC4-6680).**

John Rubens Smith and his wife Elizabeth produced a family of artists, notably their son John Rowson, who gained fame in 1848 when he completed and exhibited a vast painted panorama of the Mississippi River from the Falls of St. Anthony to the Gulf of Mexico. This view from the Pennsylvania coal mining district was engraved by the father after a drawing by the son. Another son colored the image.

VIEW OF   POTTSVILLE

Taken from Sharp Mountain & respectfully dedicated to the enterprising citizens of the COAL REGION by.

fleshy nudes from exhibition in rooms adjacent to Smith's academy.[18] He became embittered and subsequently severely criticized the Academy and its exhibitions in published reviews. A primary target of his barbs and his foremost antagonist during this period was William Dunlap, an artist better known for his enormously influential multivolume biographical history of the period, in which he belittled Smith's artistic accomplishments and harshly recalled the details of the American Academy of Art debacle. Smith's reputation as an artist never recovered.[19]

The quality and scope of works in the Smith archives gives the lie to Dunlap's unflattering account. The collection comprises almost seven hundred and fifty watercolors, drawings, prints, and some manuscript material, including prints and drawings not only by Smith, but by family members and pupils as well.[20] Smith gathered much of the material himself as a monument to his career and the accomplishments of his family. A portion of the collection was assembled for use by Smith's students as models for instruction. These items shed light on the working and teaching methods of a nineteenth-century artist, printmaker, and drawing master.[21]

Smith and his contemporaries preferred the medium of aquatint engraving to reproduce their drawn views but witnessed the early development of lithography. It was left to the ensuing generation to fully

realize the new medium's commercial potential. Philadelphia was a leading center for lithography and James Queen (1820 or 1821-1886) became one of the city's most proficient and prolific practitioners.[22] Born in Philadelphia, James Queen spent much of his time drawing scenes observed in and around the city, to develop his artistic skills and expand his inventory of images for commercial publication. He worked primarily for P. S. Duval, a pioneer in the art of lithography, who considered Queen "one of the best artists in the country."[23] The Carson Collection includes hundreds of lithographic portraits, landscapes, and street scenes drawn by him, as well as numerous pencil and watercolor sketches created during his travels through the mid-Atlantic states.

Marian Carson acquired the Queen collection from two ladies, probably when she was living in New York in the 1930s:

They lived in New Jersey, near Freehold. I realized it was a whole collection and ought to be kept together. I told the ladies I would like to buy the collection. I knew if I didn't strike they would be taking the things piece by piece to Harry Peters.[24] I put a price on a tablet and said, "This is what I'd like to pay, not a penny more or less." Then one sister said, "Get out the ice cream!"[25]

James Queen, *Fairmount Waterworks.*
Pencil on grey paper, ca. 1855-56. Prints and Photographs
Division, Library of Congress (LC-USZC4-6667).

The James Queen archives include numerous preparatory drawings
for finished works, such as these views of the Fairmount Waterworks
on the Schuylkill River above Philadelphia. The grounds of the
waterworks were turned into a public gardens and promenade,
the beginnings of Fairmount Park.

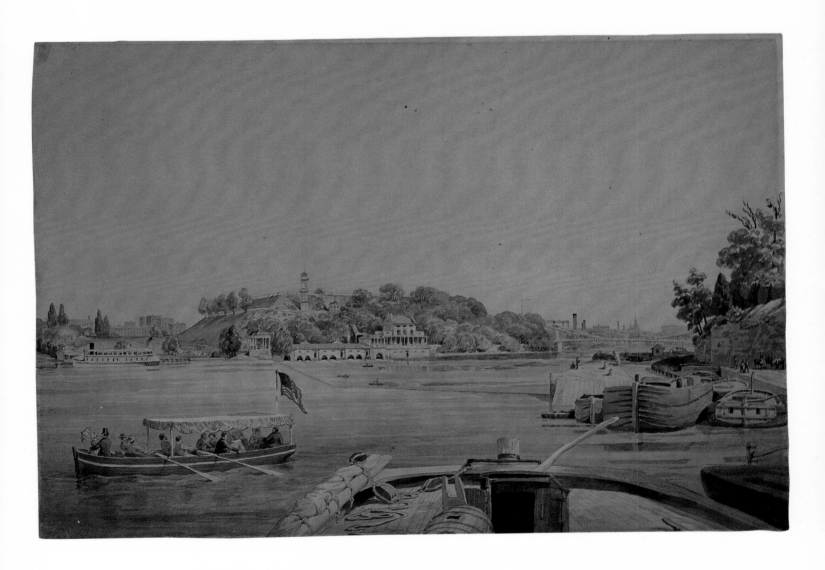

James Queen, *Fairmount Waterworks.*
Watercolor on layered paper, ca. 1856. Prints and Photographs
Division, Library of Congress (LC-USZC4-6723).

DELAWARE WATER GAP.

Like John Rubens Smith, Queen roamed the surrounding region making drawings. Unlike Smith, however, Queen devoted himself full time to drawing and found steady employment with Duval and the city's other print publishers. Along with his more scenic depictions, Queen turned out designs for certificates, bank notes, family registers, and advertisements. During the Civil War, he produced patriotic sheet music covers (see page 13), chromolithographs of hospitals, and posters advertising Sanitary Fairs. Although over forty at the time, he even served as a soldier briefly during the panic in Pennsylvania that ensued following the Confederate incursion into Maryland in mid-September 1862. Queen accompanied a Philadelphia militia company on a march toward the front and recorded their progress picturesquely in a series of watercolors preserved in the Carson Collection. He saw no action, however, and

LEFT

James Queen, *Delaware Water Gap*. Watercolor on paper, 1856. Prints and Photographs Division, Library of Congress (LC-USZC4-6678).

The picturesque topography of the Delaware Water Gap, cut by the Delaware River through Kittatinny Mountain on the New Jersey-Pennsylvania line, was a favorite motif for American artists during the nineteenth century.

RIGHT

Ibbotson & Queen after James Queen, *Delaware Water Gap*. Chromolithograph on paper, ca. 1856. Prints and Photographs Division, Library of Congress (LC-USZC4-6672).

In creating a print after his drawing of the Delaware Water Gap, James Queen replaced the summery hues of the original with a more muted autumnal palette. The imprint on this lithograph suggests Queen formed an independent printmaking partnership for a brief period.

James Queen,
Citizens Volunteer Hospital Philadelphia.
Chromolithograph on paper, ca. 1862. Prints and Photographs Division, Library of Congress (LC-USZC4-6679).
The original drawing for this chromolithograph is also in the Carson Collection. Both the drawing and print likely date from 1862, the year in which the hospital opened.

P.S. Duval after James Queen, *O.N. Thacher, Wholesale & Retail Hat, Cap & Fur Ware-House.* Lithograph with watercolor on paper, ca. 1840s. Prints and Photographs Division, Library of Congress (LC-USZC4-6673).
Queen's advertisements, adapted from sketches, engravings, daguerreotypes, ambrotypes, and plumbeotypes, provide a wealth of information about American commerce in the mid–nineteenth century. This trade card is in the same general style as others he made for Mme. Petit's French millinery, dress, and flowermaking establishment and for Hogen and Thompson's book and stationery factory and store. The lithographic printer P. S. Duval, who had been brought to Philadelphia from France by C. G. Childs and Henry Inman in 1831, worked closely with Queen for many years.

James Queen, [Church Bivouac]: *Sketches with Co B. 8th Reg. Pa. Ma. Under the officers of the Old Southwark Gaurd [sic] in Chambersburg.* Watercolor on paper, 1862. Prints and Photographs Division, Library of Congress (LC-USZC4-6675).

Just prior to the Battle of Antietam in mid-September 1862, the artist James Queen accompanied a Philadelphia volunteer militia company on a march toward the front and recorded their progress picturesquely in a series of watercolors preserved in the Carson Collection.

returned to Philadelphia with his regiment following the Rebel repulse at the Battle of Antietam.

Her combined interest in documentary drawings and the Civil War also compelled Marian Carson to acquire eighteen watercolors from the era by the artist and soldier William McIlvaine, Jr. (1813–1867). Born in Philadelphia, McIlvaine studied art, traveled abroad, and by 1845 had become a professional artist and illustrator.[26] In 1856 he relocated to New York and in the spring of 1861, at age forty-eight, responded to President Lincoln's call for soldiers to defend the Union. He enlisted as a private in Company A of the 5th Regiment New York Infantry (Colonel Abraham Duryea's Advance Guard of the New York Zouaves). He served at Fortress Monroe, Virginia, and Camp

Federal Hill, near Baltimore, at the siege of Yorktown, the Seven Days Battles, Second Bull Run, Antietam, Fredericksburg, and Chancellorsville. In February 1863, he was commissioned a second lieutenant and in May was mustered out after two years' service. He returned to Brooklyn, where he died four years later. He is remembered for his lovely, evocative watercolors of scenes encountered within the theater of war. Most of the McIlvaine watercolors in the Carson Collection images date from the 1862 Peninsular Campaign, in which Northern troops under the direction of General George McClellan pursued an ultimately futile assault on the Confederate capital at Richmond. Unlike the dramatic battle scenes drawn by newspaper sketch artists,

McIlvaine recorded moonlit views along the Chickahominy River, a sunset over the Yorktown encampment, and brightly garbed Zouaves gazing at the region's historic homes and churches from the Revolutionary and Colonial eras. The watercolors comprise a picturesque portfolio of scenic views which illustrate the peaceful interludes between the intermittent fighting that characterized the Peninsular Campaign.

Two more ephemeral items from the Civil War era complement the prints, drawings, photographs, manuscripts, and books from the period acquired by Marian Carson. Collectible comic card series were popular during the Civil War, providing amusement to the several hundred thousand troops scattered throughout the country. Ironically, ephemera by definition has only momentary value; these cards were often thrown away and are now relatively scarce. Uncut sheets constituting an entire series are rarer still. The James Queen archives includes two notable examples, the first an uncut sheet of twelve comic cards chronicling the Civil War misadventures of a reluctant rabbit recruit. Created by Henry Louis Stephens (1824-1882), one of the country's leading caricaturists and editor of the satirical journal *Vanity Fair*,[27] the Carson Collection sheet is accompanied by four of Stephens' original drawings for the set. A second important uncut sheet of cards in the collection depicts seriously and dramatically in twelve scenes the ironic journey toward freedom of an African American slave, from life on the plantation to death on a Civil War battlefield (see page 26).

Marian Carson's interest in graphic art extended to the broad genre of ephemera which encompasses tickets, stamps, bank notes, and pictorial labels and cards of various types. She filled numerous albums with bank note engravings, stock and bond certificates, trade cards, lottery and railway tickets, pictorial letterheads, and other ephemera related to finance, commerce, industry, transportation, postal history, and many other subjects. Post-Civil War technological advances created for the first time national networks in travel and communications, which accelerated the healing process and encouraged

CENTENNIAL EXHIBITION.
1876.

CENTENNIAL SOUVENIR.

INTERNATIONAL EXHIBITION,
1876.

ADMIT THE BEARER

rough Gate No. 48 to the Judges' Pavilion,

Friday, June 9th, after 7 P.M.

RESENT THIS TICKET AT THE GATE AND JUDGES' PAVILION.

JOHN BUECHLE,
HOTEL AND RESTAURANT,
No. 149 N. Front Street. PHILADELPHIA.

CENTENNIAL EXHIBITION.

PROGRAMME
-OF-
FIREWORKS

Wednesday Eve'ng, Oct. 18th, '76,

AT SEVEN O'CLOCK,
—IN THE—

Centennial Exhibition Grounds, Phila.

By Messrs. C. T. BROCK & CO., of London.

1. Grand Salute of Aerial Maroons.
2. Illumination of all the buildings, and the park appropriated for the Exhibition, covering an area of over 200 acres, during which 100 large Rockets, 50 five inch Shells, and 6 large Magnesium Balloons will make their flight, the whole forming an imposing picture.
3. Simultaneous flight of 50 five inch Shells of Turquoise and Ruby Stars.
4. An ascent of 100 brilliant Tourbillions.
5. 80 large Rockets, with twinkling Stars.
6. Great Fountain of Fire, 100 feet high.
7. Battery of 50 Mines of Saucissons.
8. 7 Flying Pigeons, flying along wires to and from their cote.
9. Representation of 2 popular Portraits, 70 ft. in width and 60 ft. high.
10. Volley of 100 eight inch Shells of every variety of color.
11. Representation of Independence Hall, 150 ft. long and 100 ft. high.
12. Volley of 100 Mines of Saucissons.
13. Simultaneous discharge of 50 ten inch Shells—"The Harlequinade."
14. Flight of 50 large Rockets, each of which will liberate twin parachutes.
15. Grand Salvo of Shells fired in rapid succession—30 eight inch, 10 ten inch, and 10 twelve inch.
16. Large Shell of Magnesium Stars.
17. Great Cascade of Fire, 210 ft. long and 100 ft. high.
18. Bouquet of 2000 large Rockets.

Admission, 50 Cts. to Exhibition and Fireworks.

☞ Special trains will leave Centennial Depots at close of the Display.

CENTENNIAL EXHIBITION. PHILADELPHIA. 1876.
CENTENNIAL DEPOT. PENNSYLVANIA R.R. CO.

TO THE
International Exhibition Co.
CENTENNIAL GROUNDS,
PHILADELPHIA, PA.

Exhibitor
Address
No. Location
Weight lbs. | No. of Packages | Serial | Total,

WILL
Open May 10th and Close November 10th.
1876.

1876.
OLYMPIC

INTERNATIONAL EXHIBITION.
AGRICULTURAL HALL.

1776 JOHN RUSSELL CUTLERY CO. 1876
NEW YORK OFFICE 97 Chambers St. AND 79 Reade St.
FACTORIES at TURNERS FALLS, MASS., U.S.A.
MANUFACTURERS OF CUTLERY.
FIRST HOME MANUFACTURERS.

JOHN G. KOEHLER,
MANUFACTURER OF
CEDAR WARE,
DEALER IN
HOUSE FURNISHING GOODS,
No. 503 NORTH SECOND ST. ABOVE NOBLE
PHILADELPHIA.

the nation's industries. By 1876, the nation's centennial, political wounds had begun to heal and Americans
were eager to display the fruits of their still fragile
union and increasingly impressive accomplishments
in the arenas of art, science, and industry. All eyes
turned toward the exposition in Philadelphia where
diverse states and trade organizations built pavilions
to promote their attractions and their wares. The
Centennial celebration represented an outburst
of nationalistic fervor and a symbolic end to decades
of intersectional rivalry, conflict, and retribution.
The Carson Collection preserves a splendid assemblage of pictorial advertising cards, admissions
tickets and passes, broadsides and placards, and
related Centennial ephemera.

These Centennial holdings, in conjunction with
photographs, books, manuscripts, and other materials
collected from the fair, represent the ultimate cogent
component of the Carson family's gathering of historical materials. Along with the substantial archives
of prints and drawings by Thomas Birch, John
Rubens Smith, and James Queen, notable works by
other American artists, and copious collections of
additional portraits, ephemera, and other graphic artifacts, they celebrate Philadelphia's central role in the
creation of the republic and document the country's
subsequent successful struggle toward the development of an enduring and unified nation.

NOTES

1. For the complicated history of Doolittle's "Display," see: Charles
Henry Hart, *Catalogue of the Engraved Portraits of Washington* (New
York, 1954), 354-57; E. McSherry Fowble, *Two Centuries of Prints in
America, 1680-1880* (Charlottesville, 1987), 317, cat. no. 212; Wendy
C. Wick, *George Washington: An American Icon* (Washington, D.C.,
1982), 35-36. There are currently at least six known states of the
print and as many as three additional variants, according to my current research and that of Doolittle biographer Donald O'Brien,
who has completed the most recent scholarship on the artist's oeuvre. Examination of the Carson Collection impression suggests that
it is a variant which falls between the states identified by Hart as
840b and 840c. As in Hart 840b, the title lettering around the portrait in the Carson impression is open with hatching, whereas the
same lettering is closed in Hart 840c. Also, Hart 840b is dated
Oct[obe]r 1st, 1791, while the Carson print is dated Mar[c]h 1st,
1794, as in Hart 840c. However Doolittle reworked the Washington
profile as seen in Hart 840c and these later changes do not appear
in the Carson impression. A variant similar to the Carson impression, but dated 1791 rather than 1794, is at this writing offered by
the Old Print Shop in New York City. Harry Newman of the Old

Print Shop has noted that their impression reveals vestiges of an
engraved map of New Jersey, which suggests an old plate was
reused for the "Display." These vestiges are referred to by Hart and
also appear in the Carson print. They offer an intriguing insight
into Doolittle's professional practice. For an account of Doolittle's
New Haven career see Reverend William A. Beardsley, "An Old
New Haven engraver and His Work: Amos Doolittle," in *Papers of
the New Haven Historical Society*, 8 (1914), 132-50.

2. Charles Hart praised the print "as being one of the largest, if not
the largest plate executed in this country at time of its issue, but
also on account of its extreme rarity." See Hart, *Catalogue of the
Engraved Portraits of Washington*, 356.

3. For the most recent and comprehensive discussion of Saint-
Mémin's work in general and the profile portrait drawing of
Washington in particular, see Ellen G. Miles, *Saint-Mémin and the
Neoclassical Profile Portrait in America* (Washington, 1994), 424, cat.
no. 922).

4. For a discussion of the five major extant sets of Saint-Mémin portrait engravings see Miles, *Saint-Mémin and the Neoclassical Profile Portrait in America*, 206-13. In 1874, the United States Congress chose not to purchase for the Library of Congress the largest extant set of 818 Saint-Mémin portraits (now preserved at the Corcoran Gallery of Art), apparently because the Library had already in 1867 acquired what is now recognized as the fifth largest set (approximately 300 engravings) with the Peter Force Collection of Americana.

5. Stan V. Henkels, *The Hampton L. Carson Collection of Engraved Portraits of Gen. George Washington* (Philadelphia, 1903), 3.

6. Hampton Carson acquired the set of Saint-Mémin portrait engravings and the memorial portrait of Washington separately. The former he purchased from Edward G. Kennedy in 1898, the latter from collector Clarence Sweet Bement of Philadelphia. See Miles, *Saint-Mémin and the Neoclassical Profile Portrait in America*, 206-13, and 424 (cat. no. 922).

7. See the list of prices realized appended to Henkels, *The Hampton L. Carson Collection of Engraved Portraits of Gen. George Washington*. For the provenance of the Saint-Mémin drawing, see Miles, *Saint-Mémin and the Neoclassical Profile Portrait in America*, cat. no. 922, 424.

8. On Mather Brown's career and oeuvre, see Dorinda Evans, *Mather Brown: Early American Artist in England* (Middletown, Connecticut, 1982). Brown's *Baptism of Edward I* is catalogue number 316, while *Brutus* is catalogue number 322. The approximate date of acquisition listed in the book for both pieces has been changed from 1935 to 1942, the year in which Joseph and Marian Carson were married.

9. On Inman's career see William H. Gerdts, *The Art of Henry Inman*, (Washington, D.C.: The National Portrait Gallery, Smithsonian Institution, 1987). The paper backing of the picture frame bears two ink inscriptions. The first reads: "Original Study in Oil by Henry Inman of Head of Columbia designed for U.S. Coins." The second, below, reads: "The above is in the handwriting of H.L.C. Acquired by J.C. at death of A.L.C. 6/22/33. Quite unique + desirable as Inman was a well known portrait painter, American, born 1801 died 1846. See Encyclopedia Britannica."

10. See Marian Sadtler Carson, "Early American Water Color Painting," in *Antiques*, LIX, no. 1 (January 1954), 54-56; also, Marian S. Carson, "The *Duncan Phyfe Shops* by John Rubens Smith, Artist and Drawing Master," in *American Art Journal*, XI, no. 4 (Autumn 1979), 69-78.

11. A similar watercolor of the same subject is in the collections of the New-York Historical Society. On Thomas Birch's life and art, see William H. Gerdts, *Thomas Birch, 1779-1851, Paintings and Drawings* (Philadelphia, 1966).

12. Although an impression has not yet been located, research files at the Pennsylvania Academy of the Fine Arts indicate that Lawson executed a print after the painting and took subscriptions for it at the Academy. Additional evidence survives on the verso of the drawing, which has retained a substantial residue of orange iron oxide powder (also known as "dragon's blood"), used by engravers to transfer an image from paper to printing plate.

13. Manuscript materials in the portfolio include Birch's citizenship papers, a copy of the 1851 auction catalogue for the posthumous sale of his studio and estate, and memorial notices composed by friend and fellow artist John Neagle and members of the Pennsylvania Academy of Fine Arts.

14. The Library acquired the John Rubens Smith collection in 1992 through a combined gift of Marian Carson and the Library's Madison Council. The collection comprises almost 750 prints and drawings from the personal archives of one of nineteenth-century America's foremost topographical artists and art instructors. The acquisition represented a milestone in the Library's history as it marked the institution's eponymous one hundred millionth accession. During a September 1996 interview, Marian Carson recalled how the collection came to be acquired by the Library: "There was a great deal of research and preservation yet to be done and I needed further help. The prints and drawings could not be lumped together. I'm not a library or a museum, I could not see running a museum out of Washington Square. That's how the collection came here [to the Library]. I noticed how beautifully you are taking care of them." These words echo Hampton Carson's published comments from ninety years previously, in which he explained his reluctant decision to disperse his collections at auction, saying the constant care they required made him "a curator of a public institution without the leisure to attend to it." See Henkels, *The Hampton L. Carson Collection of Engraved Portraits of Gen. George Washington*, 3.

15. The principal source for information on Smith's life is an unpublished manuscript biography written by his grandson Edward Sanger Smith. The biography is preserved in the manuscript collections of the New York Public Library. For an abbreviated version of this work see, Edward S. Smith, "John Rubens Smith: An Anglo-American Artist," in *Connoisseur* 85 (May 1930), 300-07; also, Frederick W. Coburn, "John Rubens Smith," in *Dictionary of American Biography* (New York, 1964) IX, 307; Museum of Fine Arts, Boston, *M. & M. Karolik Collection of American Water Colors & Drawings* (Boston, 1962) I, 275-78; and Smith's unattributed obituary in the artistic and literary review, *Crayon* (7 November 1855), 287.

16. To Smith's credit, numerous engraved and lithographic views of American cities, towns, architectural and topographic landmarks were produced after his drawings, issued separately by local printers for a more regional market. Original drawings for some of them are included in the Smith collection.

17. The *Hudson River Portfolio* was published by New York City publisher Henry Megarey between 1821 and 1825. It comprises twenty engravings (twenty-four were projected) after paintings by William Guy Wall, issued in five sets of four prints. Just prior to the project's inception, Wall had been a prized pupil of Smith's. Megarey hired Smith to engrave Wall's paintings, but after four plates had been completed Smith was replaced by John Hill (1775-1849), a skilled English printer recently arrived from London. Smith's grandson, Edward Sanger Smith, whose unpublished biography remains the most comprehensive examination of the artist's life, asserted that his grandfather conceived of the project and that he had been treated badly by Wall and Megarey. A bitter inscription by Smith in the margin of a watercolor view of New York City, included in the John Rubens Smith Collection, lends credence to the assertion: "Walls [sic] style of painting before he came to me, in a year after I got him engaged to Megary [sic]— to paint the subjects for Hudson River Portfolio—in return he gratefully tried to ruin me in Business—in gratitude J.R.S." The additional inscription, "Painted about 1825 to 1828," makes it unclear as to whether the work is by Wall, as Edward Sanger Smith asserts, or whether John Rubens Smith painted it later in derisive imitation of Wall's early style. Although the Smith Collection also includes several other drawings related to the project, until a definitive biography of Smith's career is undertaken, based in part on the materials Marian Carson preserved, we can only speculate as to the circumstances surrounding Smith's dismissal. For a discussion of the *Hudson River Portfolio*, and Smith's part in it, see William Diebold, "Four Great Sequences of Hudson River Prints," in IMPRINT, 21, no. 1 (Autumn 1995), 2-18.

18. Previous to this incident Smith and Vanderlyn were close friends and a magnificent undated watercolor view of the Hudson River by Smith bears his inscription, "Drawn in company with Mr. Vanderlyn who was dozing on the soldiers [sic] graves near the gate to Lord's Tavern, Sally Lord looking after her brothers [sic] sloop coming up."

19. See William Dunlap, *A History of the Rise and Progress of the Arts of Design in the United States*, Dover reprint edition, two volumes bound in three (New York, 1969). For passages pertinent to the Vanderlyn affair see Volume II, Part Two, 276-280; for Dunlap's brief, critical assessment of Smith's career see Volume Two, Part One, 259.

20. On the life of John Rowson Smith, Jr., see Frederick W. Coburn, "John Rowson Smith," in *Dictionary of American Biography* (New York, 1964) IX, 306-07.

21. For a description of the original assembly, gradual dispersal, and ultimate preservation of extant portions of the John Rubens Smith archives see Edward Sanger Smith, "John Rubens Smith," 75-78.

22. In 1954, University of Pittsburgh graduate student Carl Malcolm Cochran submitted an unpublished thesis on the life and work of James Queen in partial fulfillment of requirements for a Master of Arts degree. Mr. Cochran was given access to the Queen archives by Marian Carson, drew heavily from them, and appended a checklist of the collection. For his later published article drawn from the thesis see Carl M. Cochran, "James Queen[,] Philadelphia Lithographer," in *The Pennsylvania Magazine of History and Biography*, LXXXII, no. 2 (April 1958), 139-75.

23. See Nicholas Wainwright, *Philadelphia in the Romantic Age of Lithography*, (Philadelphia: Historical Society of Pennsylvania, 1958), 38.

24. Harry Peters (1881-1948) was the leading authority on, and dealer in, American popular prints at this time. His books include *Currier & Ives, printmakers to the American people* (Garden City, New York, c1929-1931) and *America on Stone: the other printmakers to the American people* (New York, c1931).

25. Interview with Mrs. Carson, September 16, 1996.

26. William P. Campbell, *The Civil War: A Centennial Exhibition of Eyewitness Drawings* (Washington, D.C., 1961), 128-29; George C. Groce and David H. Wallace, *The New-York Historical Society Dictionary of Artists in America, 1564-1860* (New Haven, 1957), 602. Additional works by McIlvaine are in the collections of the National Archives, Washington, D.C., and the Civil War Library and Museum in Philadelphia.

27. This was the shortlived *Vanity Fair* published in New York City between 1859 and 1863 not the later celebrated English and American magazines of the same name. For brief accounts of Stephens' work and career see James Grant Wislon and John Fiske, eds., *Appleton's Cyclopaedia of American Biography* (New York, 1894) V, 666; Sinclair Hamilton, *Early American Book Illustrators and Wood Engravers, 1670-1870* (Princeton, 1958), 208-210; George C. Groce and David H. Wallace, *The New-York Historical Society Dictionary of Artists in America, 1564- 1860* (New Haven, 1957), 602.

Photographic Material

by Carol Johnson

Assistant Curator of Photography, Prints and Photographs Division, Library of Congress

OPPOSITE

(detail) Mathew Brady, Portrait of William Sidney Mount. Half-plate daguerreotype, ca. 1850. See page 106.

I always looked forward to visiting Mrs. Carson in her spacious Philadelphia townhouse. Behind her front door was a magical place filled with treasures, the likes of which one usually sees only in museums. Her bookshelves, cabinets, and closets contained collections amassed not only by herself, but by several generations of her family. Over the years, Mrs. Carson welcomed many visitors to her home, often sharing the collections with historians, curators, and collectors.

I first had the pleasure of meeting Marian S. Carson in the early 1990s on one of her trips to the Library. She arrived early for a meeting and I offered to show her some of the Library's daguerreotypes.[1] We looked at several portraits from the American Colonization Society Collection, portraits of African Americans who had settled on the west coast of Africa, in Liberia. Mrs. Carson immediately expressed her interest in black history and her knowledge of Philadelphia's active role in the Colonization Society. As a matter of fact, she mentioned that she owned a watercolor of the Liberian Senate from the daguerreian era.

Shortly after her visit, Mrs. Carson sent me a small snapshot of the watercolor. The figures represented in the photograph were small and indistinct, but I was intrigued by the key (list of names) that appeared under the painting. I recognized many of the names from the daguerreotypes in the Library's American Colonization Society Collection. The painting was signed "Drawn by Robert K. Griffin, Monrovia." Ship passenger lists provided me with information about Griffin. In 1856 at the age of nineteen, Griffin had emigrated to Liberia under the auspices of the American Colonization Society. His occupation was listed as a painter.

With this piece of information, I phoned Mrs. Carson and asked if I could visit her to see the painting. A few weeks later I made my first trip to Mrs. Carson's home with copy photographs of the Library's American Colonization Society daguerreotypes in my briefcase. We took Griffin's painting off the wall and compared it to the photographs. We were both very surprised to discover that Mrs. Carson's painting was based on the daguerreotypes held by the Library. Eleven of the twelve identified sitters in the painting are represented in the Library's daguerreotype collection. Later that day, as I was getting ready to leave, Mrs. Carson spoke about the importance of keeping collections together and joked about adding the American Colonization Society daguerreotypes to her collection. Instead, Mrs. Carson kindly allowed her painting to come to the Library while I researched the relationship between her image and the Library's daguerreotypes.

On subsequent visits, I began to see the depth of

LEFT

Robert K. Griffin, The Liberian Senate. Watercolor and graphite on paper, ca. 1856. Prints and Photographs Division, Library of Congress (LC-USZC4-4908).

Nineteen-year-old Griffin painted the Liberian Senate shortly after arriving in Liberia. The painting most likely documents Edward J. Roye, standing on the left side of the room with his right hand raised, taking the oath of office as a senator. Roye had recently been elected to fill the vacancy of the late Hon. G. H. Ellis. Ellis's death could account for the black mourning cloth draped along the walls of the room.

RIGHT

Attributed to Augustus Washington, Portrait of Edward J. Roye. Sixth-plate daguerreotype, ca. 1856. American Colonization Society Collection, Prints and Photographs Division, Library of Congress (LC-USZ6-1933).

Prior to his political career, Edward J. Roye (1815-1872) operated a successful business exporting African products to England and the United States. Roye served in the Liberian government as a senator and chief justice, and was elected to the office of president. His brief term as president was marked by scandal, and he was removed from office. Roye's portrait in the watercolor [above] was clearly drawn from this laterally reversed daguerreotype.

Charles J. Wister, *Garside's Mill, Wissahickon, June 18th, 1858.* Quarter-plate ambrotype. Prints and Photographs Division, Library of Congress (LC-USZC4-6544).

A native of Germantown, Pennsylvania, Charles J. Wister experimented with both the ambrotype process and its predecessor, the daguerreotype. An ambrotype, a positive image on glass, was produced by placing a dark backing behind an underexposed glass plate negative. By the late 1850s, ambrotypes had replaced the more expensive and technically more difficult daguerreotype process.

Mrs. Carson's photographic holdings. Not one to collect the well-known masterworks of photography prized for their artistic beauty, Mrs. Carson collected images which reflected her interest in historical context, particularly photographs related to Philadelphia. Renowned for its early daguerreotypes, Mrs. Carson's collection also contains approximately 2,500 stereographs,[2] including work by the Amateur Photographic Exchange Club and two dozen early stereographs on glass; more than sixty salted-paper prints[3] of Philadelphia architecture and personalities; and subject files that include nearly one hundred and seventy-five photographs relating to topics as diverse as African American history, sports teams, labor, and transportation.

Prior to the acquisition of the Carson Collection, the strength of the Library's nineteenth-century photographic holdings began with Mathew Brady's daguerreotype portraits from the late 1840s through the 1850s. The Carson Collection, with its emphasis on early Philadelphia photography, expanded the Library's holdings to include some of the earliest American daguerreotypes, a small group of calotype negatives,[4] a large collection of salted-paper prints, and several examples of early amateur photography.

Mrs. Carson began collecting photography in the mid-1930s when very few people, let alone women,

were acquiring photographic images. Interest in historical photography grew in the 1930s, with the celebration of the centennial of photography in 1939. Two landmark publications on the history of photography were published, Beaumont Newhall's *History of Photography* (1937) and *Photography and the American Scene* by Robert Taft (1938). Mrs. Carson corresponded with both of these historians about her collection.

Mrs. Carson's interests went beyond the acquisition of objects, she was also a self-taught historian. Over one hundred and fifty American photographs from her collection were exhibited at the Smithsonian Institution in 1939, including what is believed to be the earliest extant daguerreotype portrait made in America, a self-portrait by Robert Cornelius. This was the first time that the portrait had been publicly exhibited since 1893. Mrs. Carson also loaned photographs to a centennial exhibition organized by the Pictorial Photographers of America, and held at the American Museum of Natural History in New York City.[5] In 1941 Mrs Carson wrote an article that was published in the University of Pennsylvania's *General Magazine and Historical Chronicle* entitled "Early Photography and the University."[6] This work expounded on ideas set forth in articles written by her grandfather, Julius F. Sachse, who served as the editor of the *American Journal of Photography* between 1890

Robert Cornelius, Self-portrait. Approximate quarter-plate daguerreotype, 1839. Prints and Photographs Division, Library of Congress (LC-USZ6-2174).

Robert Cornelius's 1839 self-portrait is believed to be the earliest extant American portrait photograph. Louis Jacques Mandé Daguerre's invention of a process for making "fixed" or permanent images through the action of light upon a photosensitive surface, i.e. photography, was announced to the French Academy of Sciences in August 1839. That October a young Philadelphian, Robert Cornelius, working out of doors to take advantage of the light, made this self-portrait using a box fitted with a lens from an opera glass. In the portrait Cornelius stands slightly off-center and hair askew, in the yard behind his family's lamp and chandelier store, peering uncertainly into the camera. Early daguerreotypy required a long exposure time, ranging from three to fifteen minutes, making the process nearly impractical for portraiture.

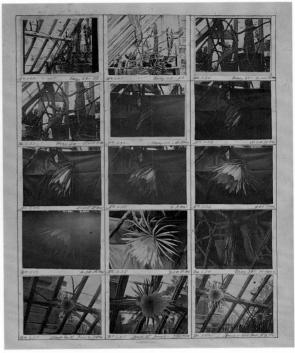

and 1897. During this time, Sachse wrote a series of articles entitled "Early Daguerreotype Days,"[7] tracing the history of the daguerreotype, with an emphasis on Philadelphia's important contributions to this field.

The foundation of Mrs. Carson's photographic collection and her first photographic acquisition was a group of daguerreotypes that once belonged to her grandfather.[8] The collection included the historically important self-portrait by Robert Cornelius. Mrs. Carson remembers seeing the Cornelius self-portrait hanging in her grandfather's home.

Sachse was an amateur photographer and historian.[9] He photographed historic sites and buildings in eastern Pennsylvania, such as the religious community, Ephrata Cloister. The interior view of the Saal (chapel) shows examples of Frakturschriften, a calligraphic art made by members of the Ephrata community.

Sachse was intrigued by the use of photography to document scientific data. In May 1888, he made a series of exposures documenting a night-blooming Cereus. These time exposures registered the growth and development of the flower. In writing about this work, Sachse stated "...no special care was taken for the purpose of making an artistic picture; the only object in view being to obtain a set of progressive plates of the gradual evolution of the bud into a flower."[10]

LEFT

Julius Sachse, *Ephrata, Interior, Widow's Saal*.
Modern gelatin silver print from the original glass plate
negative, ca. 1890. Prints and Photographs Division,
Library of Congress (LC-S1133-1).

Julius Sachse studied the German pietist sects that emigrated
to Pennsylvania during the late seventeenth century in search
of religious freedom. Concerned about the preservation of the
buildings at Ephrata Cloister, Sachse photographed these
historic structures.

RIGHT

Julius Sachse, The Evolution of the Cereus.
Cyanotype, 1888. Prints and Photographs Division,
Library of Congress (LC-USZC4-6397).

Following in her grandfather's footsteps, Mrs. Carson believed in the value to history of acquiring whole collections rather than single, rare objects. Sometimes she procured family archives, such as the John McAllister, Jr. Collection, one of the more important photography-related collections she acquired.[11] The collection contains manuscripts, photographs, books, and paper ephemera related to the McAllister family and business.

John McAllister, Jr. operated a world renowned optical shop on Philadelphia's Chestnut Street in the early 1800s, supplying spectacles to Thomas Jefferson, Henry Clay, and President Andrew Jackson. After a successful career as an optometrist, McAllister retired in 1835, turning the business over to his son, William Young McAllister. At the McAllister shop, pioneering daguerreotypist Robert Cornelius purchased the opera glass which he used as a lens for his self-portrait. An early Cornelius daguerreotype of Philadelphia's Eighth and Market Streets was displayed at the shop. This daguerreotype is unusual because the street scene is not latterly reversed, suggesting that the photographer used a prism or a mirror during the exposure.[12] William Young McAllister discussed this daguerreotype in a letter to an unknown recipient dated January 1, 1843. He states "…about using a looking glass I can say that is in common use here for views but I believe is not generally used for portraits—we have at the store a very beautiful view taken about 2 years since by Cornelius all the signs read right—that is not backward…."[13]

The McAllister family's fascination with photography is clearly evident in the collection's many daguerreotypes and paper prints documenting the family, their optical shop, and their home. Included in the collection is a daguerreotype portrait of John McAllister, Jr., the first daguerreotype taken "as a Matter of business" at Robert Cornelius's studio. In a letter reminiscing about the sitting, written in 1864 to Cornelius's partner, John Beck Goddard, McAllister wrote: "He [Cornelius] had mentioned to me, a few days before, that he had engaged a Room at the S.E. corner of Lodge St. and South 8th St., and that he would commence the business on a Certain day. When I mentioned this to Mrs. McAllister she said 'do go early on that day so that you may be the very first'—I called at the Room on the previous day, which was May 6, 1840, in order to inform Mr. C. that I would be there very early on the next morning. 'Well,' said he, 'I have all ready and if you will sit down I will take it now.' To this I readily agreed."[14]

John McAllister's son, William Young McAllister, was an early amateur photographer. By 1843 he was making daguerreotypes of his family. Unlike traditional studio portraits, William Young McAllister's daguerreotypes have a casual, snapshot quality, and yet they are technically well-executed. He photographed his father on the roof of their Chestnut Street store. This image may have been taken outdoors in order to take advantage of the light, since daguerreotypes required fairly lengthy exposure times. A year later, he captured the daily life of his family, daguerreotyping his infant son as he was taking a nap.

John McAllister, Jr. commissioned photographers to document the family's storefront and homes,

Robert Cornelius, Eighth and Market Streets, Philadelphia. Sixth-plate daguerreotype, May 1840. Prints and Photographs Division, Library of Congress (LC-USZ6-2172). This photograph by Edward Owen.

Philadelphia was one of the most daguerreotyped cities in the United States. Made in the heart of the city's commercial district, this early street scene shows a laterally correct image, indicating that the daguerreotype was taken through a mirror or a reversing prism.

Attributed to John Moran, *McAllister's Store, 728 Chestnut Street*. Albumen silver print, 1860. Prints and Photographs Division, Library of Congress (LC-USZ62-122394).

During the 1800s the McAllister family operated a world renowned optical shop on Philadelphia's Chestnut Street. John McAllister, Jr. (second from right) stands behind a table of stereoscopes, the optical instruments designed for viewing stereographs.

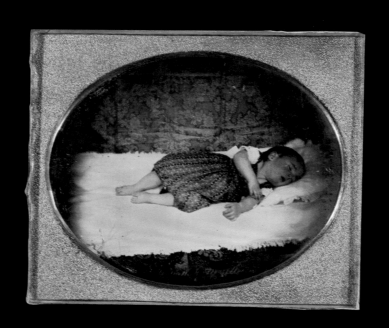

The extensive photographic documentation included with the collection provides an unusual insight into affluent Philadelphia life in the mid-1800s.

demonstrating an interest in the use of photography to record change over time. Prior to the 1843 renovation of the McAllister store, William G. Mason daguerreotyped the building so that McAllister would have a record of the original structure. A discussion of this commission is mentioned in a letter to Paul Beck Goddard: "In June 1843 McAllister & Co. concluded to modernize the first story… of the old house no. 48 Chestnut St., and to take away the shop window, which, at the time the house was built by my father (in 1794) and for many years afterwards, was the largest in the city. I wished to procure a likeness of the old front, and Mr. Mason, as by request, kindly took a daguerreotype view of it—this was on 17th June 1843."[15] The extensive photographic documentation included with the McAllister family collection provides an unusual insight into affluent Philadelphia life in the mid-1800s.

Daguerreotype portraits were a strength of Mrs. Carson's collection. In addition to the work of Robert Cornelius, the collection contains portraits of many well-known Americans, including the inventor Samuel F. B. Morse and the painter William Sidney Mount. Mathew Brady's splendid full-length portrait of Mount appears to have caught the artist just as he walked into the studio, as Mount still wears his top hat and carries his overcoat in his arms (see next page). This portrait complements the Library's Brady collection, which includes the largest collection of Brady daguerreotypes in existence.

The collection also contains many outstanding daguerreotype portraits of Philadelphia personalities, including scientists James C. Booth and Samuel

W. Woodhouse; numerous portraits of members of the Cresson family, known for their generous philanthropic activities; and a portrait of the author and labor leader, George Lippard (see next page). A nineteenth-century romantic, Lippard wrote the *The Quaker City; or, The Monks of Monk Hall*, the best selling American novel prior to Harriet Beecher Stowe's publication of *Uncle Tom's Cabin*. In 1849 Lippard founded a labor organization, the Brotherhood of the Union. A year after its founding, the Brotherhood claimed members in nineteen states and was a leading force in the cooperative movement, with the establishment of a cooperative store for Philadelphia seamstresses. Tragically, Lippard contracted tuberculosis and died shortly before his thirty-second birthday.

Among Mrs. Carson's sizable manuscript collection, it is not surprising to find a broadside advertising a dagurrean [sic] gallery.[16] Dating from 1856, the broadside for Nelson B. Vars's photographic studio was designed to attract attention with bold lettering proclaiming "FREEDOM IN KANSAS." The broadside refers to widespread interest in the debate over whether Kansas would be admitted into the union as a free or slave state (see next page).

Vars learned the daguerreotype process in 1853, while residing in New York City. In 1856 and 1857, he worked as a photographer in Mystic, Connecticut. Like many photographers of the time, Vars named a photographic process, the vareotype, after himself. Most likely, the vareotype was either a daguerreotype, an ambrotype, or a slight variation on one of these processes. The "artist" displayed nearly three hundred "pictures" in his gallery.

Unattributed, Portrait of George Lippard. Half-plate daguerreotype, ca. 1850. Prints and Photographs Division, Library of Congress (LC-USZC4-6548). This photograph by Edward Owen.

George Lippard (1822–1854), a Philadelphia novelist, social reformer, and journalist, wrote a fictional exposé of Philadelphia's élite entitled The Quaker City; or, The Monks of Monk Hall, *which became the best-selling American novel prior to Harriet Beecher Stowe's publication of* Uncle Tom's Cabin. *In 1849 Lippard founded a labor organization, the Brotherhood of the Union.*

Mathew Brady, Portrait of William Sidney Mount. Half-plate daguerreotype, ca. 1850. Prints and Photographs Division, Library of Congress (LC-USZC4-6547).

Mathew Brady's full-length portrait of the painter William Sidney Mount (1807–1868) appears to have caught the artist just as he walked into the studio, as Mount still wears his top hat and carries his overcoat in his arms. This portrait complements the Library's Brady collection, which includes the largest collection of Brady daguerreotypes in existence.

A. Watrous, *Freedom in Kansas*. Broadside for N. B. Vars Dagurrean [sic] Gallery, 1856. Rare Book and Special Collections Division, Library of Congress.

This broadside advertises a daguerreian gallery in Mystic, Connecticut. Dating from 1856, the broadside for Nelson B. Vars's photographic studio was designed to attract attention with bold lettering proclaiming "FREEDOM IN KANSAS." The broadside refers to widespread interest in the debate over whether Kansas would be admitted into the union as a free or slave state.

Frederick & William Langenheim, United States Custom House, Philadelphia. Hyalotype, ca. 1850. Prints & Photographs Division, Library of Congress (LC-USZC4-6546). This photograph by Asman Custom Photo.

A masterpiece of Greek Revival architecture, the United States Custom House was originally designed by Philadelphia-born architect William Strickland as the Second Bank of the United States. In 1832 President Jackson vetoed the bank's charter, ordering all government deposits to be withdrawn. The bank eventually failed. Between 1845 and 1935 the building served as a custom house. It was the first building purchased for Independence National Historical Park, and it now houses a permanent portrait gallery.

The daguerreotype process prevailed in the United States from its conception in 1839 to the late 1850s because the inventor of the process, Louis Jacques Mandé Daguerre, did not patent his invention in the United States. Photographers had unrestricted access to information about the daguerreotype process. However, photographic experimentation flourished during the mid-1800s, especially in Philadelphia. The commercial firm of Frederick and William Langenheim was on the forefront of new photographic techniques. Although they operated a successful daguerreotype studio, the Langenheims decided to purchase the exclusive American rights to William Henry Fox Talbot's calotype or "Talbotype" process, which used paper negatives to make multiple prints. These paper prints lacked the clarity of daguerreotypes and never became popular in the United States. The Carson Collection contains four rare Langenheim paper negatives, including one negative that may be a portrait of Mrs. Carson's great-grandfather, John Henry Friedrich Sachse.[17]

In 1848 the brothers made the first positive photographic images on glass, called "Hyalotypes," or glass lantern slides, which were projected in a magic lantern. The brothers received a medal for their Hyalotypes in 1851 at the famous Crystal Palace exhibition. Glass lantern slide shows became a popular form of entertainment and lantern slides produced by the Langenheim brothers were offered for sale at the McAllister optical shop. Frederick and William Langenheim went on to become the first American commercial stereo photographers and publishers.[18]

With the advent of glass plate negatives in the 1850s, photographers were able to make multiple prints capable of high resolution. In March 1860 John McAllister Jr. commissioned Frederick DeBourg Richards to make photographs of the McAllister home and the home of his late father.[19] Richards, a landscape painter who turned to photography in the late 1840s, had a reputation for photographing early Philadelphia buildings, many of which were being torn down and replaced with modern structures. Mrs. Carson acquired over fifty of Richards' salted-paper prints from a descendant of the photographer. His images include churches, theaters, retail establishments, private homes, and portraits of artists, actors and actresses, and firemen.

Frederick DeBourg Richards, Arch Street Theatre, Philadelphia Salted-paper print, 1850s. Prints and Photographs Division, Library of Congress (LC-USZ62-122391).

One of Philadelphia's oldest continuing theaters, the Arch Street Theatre was designed by William Strickland and opened in 1828 with a comedy, The Honeymoon; *a farce,* Three and a Deuce; *and the reading of a prize address by "a gentleman of the city." Edwin Booth made his first Philadelphia appearance at the Arch Street Theatre. In 1863 this building was demolished to make way for a new theater building.*

Frederick DeBourg Richards, Portrait of a fireman from the Perseverance Hose Company. Salted-paper print, 1850s. Prints and Photographs Division, Library of Congress (LC-USZ62-122395).

Excitement and friendship attracted many men to firefighting. Fire companies, often organized around social and political interests, were also rivals, hurrying to extinguish fires, protect property, and save lives. Firemen lacked protective clothing and communicated with speaker trumpets.

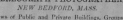

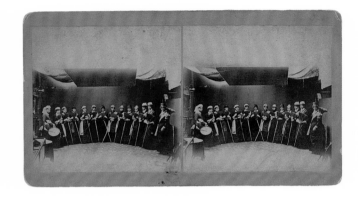

CROUP OF SHAKERS.

The largest portion of Mrs. Carson's photographic collection consists of stereographs, arranged by geographic location or by subject. The majority of the collection consists of views of Philadelphia. Other subjects include fairs and expositions, with extensive coverage of the 1876 Centennial Exposition; portraits of well-known individuals, including President William McKinley and Harriet Beecher Stowe; and images relating to war, including a group of images documenting the Russo-Japanese War.

Some of the more unusual items in the collection include a small group of stereographs depicting Shakers. Taken shortly after the Civil War, these images document the Shakers at a critical period in the sect's history, when its population was declining. James Irving of Troy, New York, took one of these photographs at the Shaker community in Mount Lebanon, New York, the center of the Shaker movement, and one of approximately twenty Shaker societies.

Shakers withdrew from society and formed a celibate community, with members living, working, and worshiping together, although men and women slept in separate dormitories. Men and women held equal roles in the community. The Shakers were interested in photography and sold stereoscopic views of their community to the public. Only 350 individual stereoscopic views of Shakers are known to exist; however none of these images were held by the Library prior to the acquisition of the Carson Collection.

In addition to commercially produced stereographs, Mrs. Carson's collection contains nearly one hundred images made by members of the first organized amateur photography groups in the United States, the Amateur Photographic Exchange Club and the Pennsylvania Photographic Society. The Amateur Photographic Exchange Club was founded in 1861 by Henry T. Anthony, whose brother operated a well-known photographic supply house in New York City. According to the club's rules, each member

TOP LEFT

Thomas Edward Mullikin White, Business Card of T.E.M. White. Albumen silver stereograph, ca. 1870. Prints and Photographs Division, Library of Congress (LC-USZ62-122401).

Thomas E. M. White (1834–1909) worked as a photographer in New Bedford, Massachusetts, during the 1870s. This stereograph cleverly serves as an advertisement for his photographic business.

TOP RIGHT

Simon Towle, Group of Women. Albumen silver stereograph, ca. 1873. Prints and Photographs Division, Library of Congress (LC-USZ62-122397).

Simon Towle's photographic studio was located in Lowell, Massachusetts. Mrs. Carson titled this image "Women's Committee, 1873." We have not yet identified this committee. Perhaps the photograph commemorates Massachusetts' adoption of a ten-hour workday for women. This stereograph is just one of many images from the Carson Collection that provide research opportunities for scholars.

BOTTOM

James Irving, *Group of Shakers*. Albumen silver stereograph, ca. 1870. Prints and Photographs Division, Library of Congress (LC-USZ62-122400).

This image was made at the Shaker community in Mount Lebanon, New York.

was required to forward at least one stereoscopic print to the other members on or before the fifteenth of every other month. The photographs were to be labeled with the name of the artist, a descriptive title, and the date of the printing. In addition, the photographs were to be guaranteed not to fade for two years.[20] In the 1860s photography was an expensive and technically challenging activity, not often pursued by amateurs. Membership included over twenty amateurs, including Charles F. Himes, a scientist and professor of mathematics at Troy University in Troy, New York; Robert Shriver, a bookkeeper from Cumberland, Maryland; and Coleman Sellers, an engineer from Philadelphia. The Club gave members a chance to discuss issues such as the advantages of dry-plate negatives over wet-plate negatives. The Amateur Photographic Exchange Club folded in 1863 when photographic supplies became scarce due to the Civil War.[21]

Always interested in unusual, historic images, Mrs. Carson occasionally purchased photographs at auction. In 1970 she purchased a few lots from the famous Sidney Strober auction at Parke-Bernet Galleries.[22] Instead of purchasing work by photographic masters such as William Henry Jackson and Carleton Watkins, Mrs. Carson bid on groups of photographs which included images that appealed to her subject interests. She was the high bidder for an assortment of group portraits, which included a riveting portrait of ten men from Watertown, New York's Division 289 of the Ku Klux Klan. Mrs. Carson filed this group portrait in a box along with a variety of manuscripts, stereographs, and other pictorial material relating to black history. The portrait dates from the late 1860s or early 1870s, shortly after the Klan was organized. Usually associated with the South, the Ku Klux Klan may have been organized in Watertown, New York, in response to an influx of Canadian workers.

Nineteenth-century images of sports teams and recreational activities, such as bowling and croquet, are represented in the Carson Collection. One of the more unusual pieces is a unique maquette of the Bachelor Baseball Club (BBBC), accompanied by a copy photograph of the piece. The maquette is made up of thirteen original carte de visite photographs cleverly placed within the hand-drawn BBBC design. The BBBC was one of the many early amateur teams based in Philadelphia. Baseball's popularity surged after the Civil War. Games attracted thou-

Hart, *Ku Klux Klan, Watertown Division 289.* Albumen silver print, ca. 1870. Prints and Photographs Division, Library of Congress (LC-USZ62-122392).

Robert Shriver, *Baltimore St., Cumberland, after a snow storm, April 10, 1862.* Albumen silver stereograph. Prints and Photographs Division, Library of Congress (LC-USZ62-122399 and LC-USZC4-6651).

Robert Shriver (1837–1912), a banker from Cumberland, Maryland, was a member of the Amateur Photographic Exchange Club. Shriver exchanged views of Cumberland and the surrounding area with other members. His younger brothers and sisters looked forward to viewing the images of New York and Philadelphia sent by members of the club.

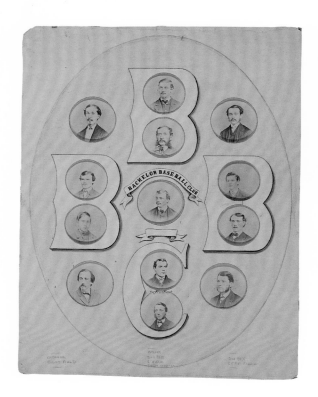

Theo. E. Peiser, Seattle's first street car turning from Occidental Avenue to Yesler Way. Albumen silver print, 1884. Prints and Photographs Division, Library of Congress (LC-USZ62-122398).

sands of spectators and an inning-by-inning summary of the action often appeared on the front page of local newspapers.

Photographic views of American life in the nineteenth century were scattered throughout Mrs. Carson's subject files. An 1884 street scene in Seattle, Washington, depicts the official opening party of the city's first street car (see also back end papers). Frank Osgood, newly arrived from Boston, planned the horse-drawn trolley route up Second Avenue. Osgood is standing behind the horse; an African American, George W. Williams, is driving the car; and three Chinese men can be seen in the foreground (many Chinese laborers worked on local railroad construction projects and in the mines). The original plan had called for the trolleys to be pulled by one horse, but it took two horses to pull the cars up some of Seattle's hills. Osgood's budget included feed for only one horse per trolley, so, realizing that the street car's operating expenses were higher than expected, he turned his interests to replacing the horse-drawn cars with electric cars. On March 31, 1889, Seattle became the first city west of the Mississippi to operate an electric railway.

Today, nearly sixty years after Marian S. Carson began to collect photography, the images that she acquired tell a fascinating story of American life in the nineteenth century. Over the years, the photographs in the Carson Collection have inspired important exhibitions and publications, resulting in new scholarship in the field. Now that this outstanding collection is part of the "American Memory" at the Library of Congress, it will continue to engage scholars for years to come.

1. Daguerreotypes were the first commercially available photographic process in the United States. This direct positive process, made on a copper plate coated with silver, produced highly detailed, mirror-like images.

2. A stereograph is a pair of photographic images mounted side by side that, when seen through a special viewer, appear three-dimensional.

3. Salted-paper prints are the earliest photographic prints on paper. The process initially utilized a paper negative, or calotype, capable of producing an unlimited number of photographic prints. Later, glass plate negatives were used. The photographic support, usually a sheet of drawing paper, was sensitized by immersion in a solution of table salt, and then coated on one side with silver nitrate. After the paper dried, the negative and sensitized paper were placed in a printing frame and exposed to sunlight until the print had achieved the desired density. In order to stop development, the print was fixed with sodium thiosulfate.

4. Prior to the acquisition of the Carson Collection, the Library's collection did not include any calotype negatives.

5. A seven-page checklist of this exhibition is included in the Carson Collection.

6. Marian Sadtler Hornor, "Early Photography and The University," *The General Magazine and Historical Chronicle*, Vol. XLIII (January 1941), 144-153 (Mrs. Carson's first husband was William Macpherson Hornor, Jr.).

7. Julius Sachse's articles on the daguerreotype appeared in the *American Journal of Photography* beginning in June 1892.

8. Julius Sachse died in 1919. Mrs. Carson was a teenager at this time. Her aunt, Emma F. Sachse, gave her part of his collection in the 1930s.

9. For more information about Julius Sachse see Marcy Silver Flynn, "Amateur Experiences: Julius Sachse and Photography," *Pennsylvania History: A Journal of Mid-Atlantic Studies* (Spring 1997), 333-348.

10. Julius F. Sachse, "The Evolution of the Cereus," *American Journal of Photography*, Vol. 9 (November 1888), 288-294.

11. Mrs. Carson acquired the McAllister Collection from Janet McAllister. Carson interview, Library of Congress, September 16, 1996.

12. Being a direct positive process, early daguerreotypes were typically mirror images of their subjects.

13. William Young McAllister to an unidentified recipient, January 1, 1843. The Marian S. Carson Collection, Library of Congress, Manuscript Division.

14. John McAllister, Jr. to Paul Beck Goddard, March 15, 1864. Marian S. Carson Collection, Library of Congress, Manuscript Division. Additional text from this letter appears in Will F. Stapp, "Robert Cornelius and the Dawn of Photography," in *Robert Cornelius: Portraits from the Dawn of Photography* (Washington: Smithsonian Institution Press, 1983), 36. Cornelius's portrait of John McAllister, Jr. is in the Carson Collection, LC DAG. no. 1256.

15. John McAllister, Jr. to Paul Beck Goddard, June 1843. Marian S. Carson Collection, Library of Congress, Manuscript Division. This daguerreotype is included in the Carson Collection, LC DAG. no. 1273.

16. The broadside is stored in the Library's Rare Book and Special Collections Division.

17. John Henry Friedrich Sachse (1803-1886) emigrated to the United States from Hanover, Germany, in 1834 and was a designer in Robert Cornelius's shop.

18. John S. Waldsmith, *Stereo Views: A Collector's Guide with Prices for Vintage Stereoviews, Tru-Views, View-Masters, and Other 3-D Visual Collectibles* (Radnor, Pennsylvania, 1991), 44.

19. Kenneth Finkel, "Vintage Views of Historic Philadelphia: Antiquarian Photography, 1853-70," in *Nineteenth Century*, 6 (Summer 1980), 56.

20. Coleman Sellers, E.D., Inst. C.E. "An Old Photographic Club," *Anthony's Photographic Bulletin*, 19 (June 8, 1888), 338-341.

21. Waldsmith, *Stereo Views: A Collector's Guide with Prices for Vintage Stereo Views*, 65.

22. The Strober auction was held at Parke-Bernet Galleries in New York on February 7, 1970. It is considered to be the first important photography auction, signaling a new interest in collecting photographs.

Index

OPPOSITE

(detail) "A-B-C Fibel. Julius Sachse. 1846." See page 5.